GAME *of* LOANS

GAME *of* LOANS

The Rhetoric and Reality of Student Debt

Beth Akers and Matthew M. Chingos

PRINCETON UNIVERSITY PRESS

PRINCETON AND OXFORD

Requests for permission to reproduce material from this work should be sent to Permissions, Princeton University Press
Published by Princeton University Press, 41 William Street, Princeton, New Jersey 08540
In the United Kingdom: Princeton University Press, 6 Oxford Street, Woodstock, Oxfordshire OX20 1TR
press.princeton.edu

Jacket art: (1) Coins courtesy of Shutterstock, (2) Mortarboard courtesy of John Kuczala/Getty Images

Library of Congress Cataloging-in-Publication Data

Names: Akers, Beth, 1983– author. | Chingos, Matthew M., 1983– author.
Title: Game of loans : the rhetoric and reality of student debt / Beth Akers and Matthew M. Chingos.
Description: Princeton : Princeton University Press, [2016] | Includes bibliographical references and index.
Identifiers: LCCN 2016022175 | ISBN 9780691167152 (hardcover : acid-free paper)
Subjects: LCSH: Student loans—United States. | Students—United States—Finance, Personal. | College graduates—United States—Finance, Personal.
Classification: LCC LB2340.2 .A54 2016 | DDC 371.2/24—dc23 LC record available at https://lccn.loc.gov/2016022175

British Library Cataloging-in-Publication Data is available

This book has been composed in Minion Pro and Lucida Std

Printed on acid-free paper. ∞

Printed in the United States of America

10 9 8 7 6 5 4 3 2 1

Contents

Acknowledgments

We are grateful to a number of individuals whose help benefited this book in many ways, both large and small. The research underlying this book was completed while we were both scholars in the Brown Center on Education Policy at the Brookings Institution, where we were fortunate to work with terrific colleagues. We thank Russ Whitehurst for his exceedingly able direction of the center and Ellie Klein and Katharine Lindquist for exceptional research assistance. Liz Sablich read the first draft of the entire manuscript and provided much useful feedback.

We are also in the debt of several individuals outside of Brookings who contributed to this effort. We made significant revisions—and corrected more than one error—in response to helpful feedback from Sandy Baum and an anonymous reviewer, both of whom read the full manuscript. Sandy Baum also shared historical data on financial aid that we use in chapter 3.

Jason Delisle, Sara Goldrick-Rab, Janet Hansen, Brad Hershbein, Robert Kelchen, Andrew Kelly, Adam Looney, and Katherine Sydor generously contributed their expertise in response to questions that arose while we were writing.

Seth Ditchik originally suggested that we write this book. He and his team at Princeton University Press did a superb job throughout the editorial process.

Additionally, Beth Akers thanks her colleagues at the Brookings Institution for thoughtful conversations, feedback, and support throughout the development of this project. Matthew Chingos thanks his colleagues at the Urban Institute, especially Greg Acs, Kristin Blagg, and Marge Turner, for their assistance and support during his first several months at Urban, which coincided with the final months of this book project.

We could not have written this book without the contributions of these individuals and the support of our families and friends. We gladly subscribe to the tradition of accepting responsibility for any errors that remain.

GAME *of* LOANS

1

A Brief Introduction to Student Loans

> Student borrowing to pay the costs of postsecond-
> ary education has skyrocketed in the last decade....
> Growing student indebtedness has raised questions
> about the implications of debt burdens for the
> national economy, for the individual well-being of
> borrowers, for equality of access to higher educa-
> tion, and even for the educational process itself.[1]

These words capture the prevailing public narrative around
student loan debt, with increasing borrowing levels raising
alarm among students, parents, policymakers, and the public.
But these concerns are not new—the passage above is from a
1986 report commissioned by the Joint Economic Committee
in the U.S. Congress. As of that writing, annual student borrowing had quintupled from a decade prior, to about $22 bil-
lion in today's dollars, or $2,400 per student.

Those borrowing levels pale in comparison to those seen
today. Over the course of the following three decades, annual
borrowing quintupled yet again, to more than $100 billion, or
about $7,000 per student.[2] The seemingly never-ending in-
creases in debt levels have aroused similar concerns about the
impact of debt on borrowers and the nation. Student loans
have become a scapegoat for a host of problems ranging from

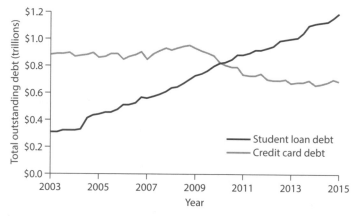

Figure 1.1. Total outstanding student loan debt and credit card debt, 2003–15 ($ Trillions)
Source: Federal Reserve Bank of New York 2015 Q1 Report. *Notes:* 2014 dollars.

a weak economic recovery to delayed marriage and child-bearing to decreases in entrepreneurship.[3]

The last decade has seen especially large increases in student debt, with two key moments attracting significant attention: total outstanding student debt surpassed total credit card debt in 2010 and then passed the $1 trillion mark in 2013, according to data assembled by the Federal Reserve Bank of New York (figure 1.1).[4] Other estimates date the passing of the $1 trillion mark as early as late 2011.[5]

The opening quote, drawn from a 1986 report titled "Student Loans: Are They Overburdening a Generation?," makes clear that fears of a student loan crisis are not new. But public attention to student loan debt has surged in recent years. Figure 1.2 shows that coverage of this topic in the *New York Times* reached an all-time high in 2014, and that in recent years it

Figure 1.2. Percentage of *New York Times* articles mentioning student loans, 1955–2014
Source: Chronicle (http://chronicle.nytlabs.com/)

has gained levels of attention last seen in the early 1980s, when crackdowns on delinquent borrowers and political fights over the loan program garnered public attention.[6]

Perhaps surprisingly, the 1986 report commissioned by the U.S. Congress found little evidence to support all of the hysteria around student loans:

> [S]ome frequently-heard concerns about student borrowing are not supported by the evidence available to date, although the paucity of good data and studies make it unwise to dismiss these concerns out of hand. In particular, it is not yet clear that high debt levels are causing serious problems for many students; that educational, career, and personal decisions are being affected by indebtedness; or that the growth in student borrowing poses a threat to the national economy.[7]

The purpose of this book is to examine whether reality has caught up with the hype and fear generated by student loans. In short, we find that it hasn't. There is no evidence of a widespread, systemic student loan crisis, in which the typical borrower is buried in debt for a college education that did not pay off. The crisis that permeates public discussion is a manufactured narrative based largely on anecdotes, speculation, shoddy research, and inappropriate framing of the issue.

The problem with this false narrative is that it makes it harder to fix the real problems in student lending. There is not a single student loan crisis, but there are many crises, ranging from the fact that most students have no more than a vague idea of how much they've borrowed, to the hundreds of thousands of borrowers needlessly defaulting on their student loans, to the pockets of students who are making decisions that lead to predictably bad completion and repayment outcomes. These are pressing problems that need solutions, but unfortunately the myth of a broad-based loan crisis has led to well-intentioned but poorly targeted policy proposals aimed at all borrowers, which work to the benefit of those with the most debt rather than those in the greatest distress.

Accurately assessing the state of student lending today requires an understanding of why student loans exist in the first place, and why they are largely made by the federal government. The remainder of this chapter develops this rationale, which provides a set of basic principles that are useful to keep in mind as we examine borrowing levels (chapter 2), trends in borrowing over time (chapter 3), the financial well-being of borrowers (chapter 4), and the possible impact of education debt on the economy (chapter 5).

We return to this set of ideas in chapter 6 by viewing the facts about student lending in the United States through the lens introduced in this chapter. The stark contrast between how student lending is supposed to work and how it works today identifies several important problems facing student lending in the United States. We conclude in chapter 7 by proposing a comprehensive set of reforms to bring reality closer to this ideal.

HOW STUDENT LOANS ARE DIFFERENT

The national dialogue about student debt often compares education loans to credit card debt. In fact, there was quite a stir in the media when total outstanding education debt surpassed total outstanding credit card debt. But it's important, for both individuals and policymakers, to recognize that student debt is different. First, let's go back to basics.

What is debt? Debt is a tool that enables an individual to consume more today by taking money from her future self. Of course, we can't travel through time to interact with our future selves, so we rely on a third party, the lender, to make this transaction possible. In practice, a loan is an agreement between a borrower and a lender, but it's important to bear in mind that a loan actually is a transaction between an individual and her future self.

There are a number of instances when taking on debt is a reasonable thing to do. For example, it makes sense to borrow when you expect that your future self will be much wealthier than your present self. It also makes sense to borrow when you make a purchase that will benefit your future self. For instance, the price tag for a new car is due when you drive the car off the lot, but the benefits of owning that car will be enjoyed over a number of years. The prevalence of borrowing to finance car and home purchases suggests that many people are comfortable using debt in this way.

But we're all familiar with the fact that many people also use debt in less constructive ways. In particular, many fall into the habit of using debt, particularly credit cards, to purchase items that they simply cannot afford—not now and not in the future. This use of debt essentially amounts to postponing the inevitable of having to cut back. We've all been warned against the pitfall of using debt to finance purchases that we can't really afford, but rhetoric would suggest that it is still a prevalent behavior.

Student debt, however, is different. Financing a college degree does not amount to the postponement of an expense that one simply cannot afford. Instead, it's a means for transferring wealth from a future period of relative prosperity to the present. Not only does this allow consumers to smooth their consumption over time, as economists put it, but the debt in itself is what generates the opportunity for the heightened future prosperity. This is to say that student debt finances an investment that pays dividends in the future rather than simply consumption that pays dividends in the present.

Many big-ticket purchases combine both consumption and investment. A prominent example is home buying, for which most Americans use mortgage financing, typically over 30 years. Home ownership is consumption if the owner lives in the home. More expensive homes generally imply greater consumption, as the owner pays more for mortgage, taxes, and the like. But houses also potentially increase in value over time, so they are also an investment. Of course buying a home based on expectations about its future value can lead to trouble, as the recent mortgage crisis made clear.

Education, like a home, is a combination of investment and consumption. College is an investment because it is expected to increase students' future incomes, on average. The consumption component of college includes all of the costs that are not strictly part of the experience that leads to a higher future income. The part of tuition that pays for beautiful leafy campuses, extracurricular activities, student centers, and athletics facilities are consumption to the extent that these expenditures do not increase what students can expect to earn after they graduate. The particular combination of investment and consumption obviously varies widely across campuses, with some looking like summer camps that offer college classes and others offering a more bare-bones experience.

In practice, it is difficult or even impossible to parse educational services in this way. Many parts of an educational experience could be classified as both consumption and investment. For example, extracurricular activities might combine learning and enjoyment. Even when it is clear that a particular aspect of college won't yield financial dividends in the future, students generally can't refuse to pay for it and generally have no way of knowing how much of their tuition it represents.

It is still worthwhile to think about the distinction between consumption and investment when one is shopping for college because colleges vary in the consumption amenities that they offer. Prospective students can refuse to pay for fancy athletic facilities and dormitories by attending a lower-priced campus that offers fewer such amenities. Students should think of student loans that pay for the consumption part of the college experience in the same way they think about credit card debt. It enables them to enjoy something right away, but they will have to pay for it later.[8] Education loans taken out to finance another person's education can also be seen in a similar light, since the borrower may not have any claim on the future earnings of the loan recipient.[9]

WHY GOVERNMENT INVOLVEMENT IN HIGHER EDUCATION?

A number of factors in the arena of higher education contribute to what economists call a market failure. This means that the natural conditions are such that the market outcome—the outcome that would occur without any government intervention—is worse than the outcome that could be achieved with the help of some well-crafted policy interventions. In the absence of government intervention, too few students would enroll in college and complete degrees, which would reduce the capacity for productivity and innovation in the nation's economy.

One important driver of this market failure in higher education comes from the fact that there are significant public returns to investments in higher education. This means that if individuals and the market were left to their own devices, public investment in higher education would be less than optimal from a societal perspective. Government subsidies to higher education serve to ensure that students from all walks of life have access to the opportunity afforded by higher education, but also serve to encourage higher levels of educational attainment across the board.

A second key failure in the market for higher education financing is the fact that student loans finance the purchase of a service, not a good. A loan used to buy a car or a house is guaranteed in part by the good itself. If the borrower fails to pay, the lender can repossess the car or foreclose on the house. There is no such collateral for a student loan. If the student fails to pay, the lender can try to get them to make good on their promise to pay, but there is no tangible object that they can take to help cover their loss on the loan gone bad. A student who wants to borrow to go to college is asking to be given money based on a promise to pay out of future income, with no collateral for the lender to take if the borrower fails to pay. A loan based on future income is riskier than a loan based on current income, and a loan without collateral is riskier than a loan with one. As a result, lenders face greater risk in making student loans, and have to charge higher prices (interest rates) to make up for it.

The upshot is that the private market will not make student loans available on attractive terms to as many borrowers as society would like to see able to borrow for college. This idea goes back to at least Milton Friedman, who in 1955 wrote about the greater risk of lending for "human capital" (education and training) than for "physical capital," and about the risk inherent in lending based on expectations of future income.[10] Friedman's proposed solution to this problem, in which borrowers make payments based on their incomes, is an idea called income share agreements that we'll return to in chapter 7.

Government intervention in the market for higher education and student loans is entirely justified on the grounds of these market failures, but it is also the case that the government has some comparative advantage when it comes to administering student loans. For instance, the government has tools to enforce repayment that the private sector does not have, such as the ability to take delinquent borrowers' wages and tax refunds. Additionally, the government can withstand a riskier loan portfolio because, unlike private lenders, it doesn't need to worry about going out of business.

THE IDEAL STUDENT LENDING SYSTEM

What does the rationale for student loans in general, and government loans in particular, tell us about what a well-functioning student lending system should look like? We identify five main features, all of which are predicated on the notion that borrowing for college should be treated as an investment decision. Education is about much more than financial success, but it should be thought of primarily as an investment for the purposes of making financial decisions that have long-term consequences for borrowers and society.

First, student loans should finance investments and not consumption to the greatest extent possible. This is especially true of government loans, for which taxpayers are taking on risk. Students and parents who want to borrow for consumption can do that in the private market, but that activity should be kept separate from what we are calling "student loans."

Second, students and their families should make well-informed decisions when determining how much to borrow. They should use the best available information on how much they will pay for their education, the chances that they will successfully earn a degree, and the income that they can expect after graduation. Taking on student debt without carefully considering these factors would be like borrowing to start a business without any idea about whether it will be successful.

Third, students should be protected from the risk inherent in borrowing to pay for their education. Students should not be allowed to make predictably bad decisions, such as borrowing to earn a degree with very low success rates or labor market prospects. In other words, students should not be able to take on significant debt if it is obvious from the outset that they will never be able to pay it back.

Fourth, not all bad loans are the result of predictably bad decisions. Some students simply get unlucky, such as by graduating in a bad economy or realizing that their chosen field is not a good fit for them (and then switching to a field with lower earnings despite having borrowed expecting higher earnings). A well-functioning lending system will protect stu-dents from this unpredictable risk.

Finally, government student lending programs should be cost-effective and protect taxpayers to the greatest extent possible. Just because the government is in a stronger posi-tion to make risky loans than the private sector doesn't mean it should do so at every opportunity. The government has a responsibility to balance its role as a steward of taxpayer dol-lars with its mission to spend those dollars to further the so-cial good.

The chapters that follow show how the student lending sys-tem in the United States falls short on all of these dimensions. At the same time, the average college student is making a good investment that will more than pay for itself over the student's lifetime. The rest of this book reconciles the overheated rhet-oric of a systemic student loan crisis with the reality that stu-dent lending suffers from real problems. These problems are too often lost in the prevailing public narrative about student debt, but solving them would make higher education more efficient and fair for all Americans.

What Does Student Borrowing in the United States Really Look Like?

The typical borrower in news stories about student loan debt has an enormous balance, is unemployed or working a low-paying job, and often lives with his parents to save money on living expenses.[1] These struggling borrowers are real, and their problems are troubling, but they are outliers in the broader picture of student borrowing in the United States. A 2014 analysis of 100 recent news stories about student debt found that the borrowers profiled had an average debt in excess of $85,000, nearly three times the average borrowing of college graduates with debt.[2] Given the prevailing media coverage, it's unsurprising that many people are confused.

What does the typical student borrower look like? In many ways, no borrower is typical. How much debt a student leaves college with is a result of both circumstances and choices. Circumstances include students' financial ability to pay for college out of their own pockets and with the help of their parents and other family members. Choices include the price of the college they choose to attend, how long they remain enrolled, and how they pay for college. A pair of identical twins attending the same college for four years could leave with different amounts of debt because of choices such as how much to work during the school year, whether to spend the summer pursuing paid or non-paid opportunities, and how much to spend on non-essentials.

Circumstances can undoubtedly constrain choices. A student from a low-income family, or with a family of her own, may have to work as much as possible just to get by. Debt is a tool that can be used to relax these constraints, enabling students to focus on their studies and then pay later when they have turned their attention to working. But debt is a double-edged sword in that it expands both the good and bad decisions students can make. A student attending a low-quality program that is unlikely to lead to a good job can borrow just as much as any other student from the federal government, which makes most student loans. This is a feature of the federal lending program that is intended to promote college access for all students, regardless of income, but has the unfortunate side effect of enabling bad investments.

There are almost as many patterns of borrowing as there are student borrowers. But although no borrower is typical, some borrowers are certainly more typical than others. The typical media anecdote, a borrower with a balance of $85,000, has more debt than 99 percent of four-year degree holders and 78 percent of graduate degree holders.[3] But the much lower average borrowing amounts mask significant variation in how much different kinds of students borrow as well as in how strong a position they are in to repay their debt.

In this chapter, we provide a broad overview of student borrowing in the United States today, including who borrows, the federal programs through which most borrowing occurs, and what the distributions of borrowing and outstanding debt look like.

THE BIG PICTURE

Students in the United States collectively took out about $100 billion in loans during the 2013–14 school year, with 90 percent coming from the federal government and the remainder from private and other sources.[4] As of this writing (end of 2015), there is $1.2 trillion in outstanding federal debt held by 42 million borrowers, which reflects borrowing in both recent and earlier years that has not yet been repaid.[5] Including private and other loans brings the total to approximately $1.3 trillion.[6]

Student debt is used to finance a wide variety of educational experiences, ranging from certificates earned in a year at open-access institutions to graduate degrees pursued over several years at elite research universities. The media narrative in which everyone is drowning in debt is misleading not just because it gets the average balance wrong but because it tends to focus on a single type of college student: someone who went straight from high school to college (and perhaps to graduate school) and then moved back home when their loan payments came due and they couldn't get a well-paying job. But students who attend college shortly after high school and meet a handful of other requirements to be considered financially "dependent" on their parents constitute less than half of all undergraduates, with the majority consisting of older "independent" students who are more likely to attend part-time, work full-time, and have families of their own.[7]

Graduate students form a third group who complicate discussions of student loans because they are more likely to have large balances, accumulated from both undergraduate and graduate programs, but they also include many highly paid professionals such as doctors and lawyers. At the same time, not all expensive graduate programs have significant value in the labor market, as media accounts of art students with $88,000 in debt make clear.[8]

These three groups of borrowers—dependent undergraduates, independent undergraduates, and graduate students— are hardly uniform, as the lawyer vs. art student comparison indicates. But they represent a useful way to divide student lending into somewhat more uniform segments, as figure 2.1 does for federal loans made in 2013–14. Graduate students only make up 14 percent of American students, but they took out 34 percent of the $90 billion in student loans made by the federal government in 2013–14. Independent undergraduates accounted for significantly more federal borrowing than dependent undergraduates (38 vs. 28 percent), despite the two groups being similar in size.

Students in each of these three segments of the market for student loans vary in their borrowing behavior because they have underlying differences, such as how much support their parents provide, and also because they face different rules in terms of how much they can borrow. In the next section, we describe federal student lending policy before turning to our examination of how much students borrow. We focus on fed-

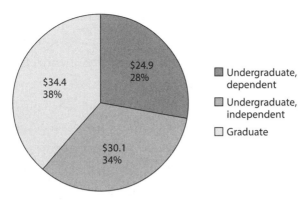

Figure 2.1. Federal loans disbursed in 2013–14 ($ billions)
Source: Authors' calculations from aggregated Federal Student Aid institution-level disbursement data. *Notes:* 2014 dollars.

eral loans to students since they constitute the bulk of student lending in the country, but also briefly discuss private student debt as well as education loans made to parents.

FEDERAL STUDENT BORROWING

The current system of federal student lending is a hodgepodge of programs that resulted from more than 50 years of policy-making, as we document in the next chapter. Loans are available to pretty much any college or graduate student who is enrolled at least half-time at an accredited institution.[9] The key feature of federal student loans is that, unlike loans made in the private sector, they are made to anyone regardless of their anticipated ability to repay. Students obtain federal loans by filling out the Free Application for Federal Student Aid (FAFSA), but the information that they provide only affects some particulars, such as whether the government pays the interest on their loans while they are in school (this is done for undergraduate students with greater demonstrated financial need).[10] The loan money is disbursed by the government to schools, who use it to pay tuition bills and then provide any remaining funds to students to cover expenses not charged by the school (such as books and living expenses).

The amount that students can borrow and the interest rates that they pay are different for dependent undergraduates, independent undergraduates, and graduate students. These terms are summarized in table 2.1 for loans made during the 2015–16 academic year.[11] Independent undergraduates can generally borrow more than dependent students, because they are presumed to be receiving less help from their families, but the two groups face the same interest rates. Undergraduates pay an interest rate of 4.29 percent on loans taken out in 2015–16, a rate that is fixed for the life of the loan.[12]

Undergraduate students generally cannot accumulate enormous amounts of federal debt.[13] A dependent student who borrows the federal maximum every year for four years would accumulate $27,000 in debt; for independent students the total is $45,000. Many students take five or six years to complete a four-year degree, but cannot borrow more than the lifetime limit of $31,000 for dependent students and $57,500 for independent students.

For graduate students, all bets are off when it comes to total borrowing. Graduate students can borrow under the same Stafford program as undergraduates, but their limits are much higher ($20,500 per year) and they can also borrow up to the

Table 2.1. **Federal Student Loan Terms, 2015–16**

	Annual Limit			Lifetime Limit	Interest Rate	Fee
	Fresh.	Soph.	Jrs./Srs.			
Under-graduate, dependent*	$5,500	$6,500	$7,500	$31,000	4.29%	1.07%
Under-graduate, independent	$9,500	$10,500	$12,500	$57,500	4.29%	1.07%
Graduate**	Cost of attendance less other aid			None	5.84%, 6.84%	1.07%, 4.29%

Source: http://ticas.org/content/posd/federal-student-loan-amounts-and-terms
-loans-issued-2015-16.
*Dependent students whose parents are unable to obtain PLUS loans can borrow up to the annual and lifetime limits for independent students.
**The more favorable terms for graduate students apply to the Stafford portion of their loans, which have an annual limit of $20,500 and a lifetime limit of $138,500. The less favorable terms apply to Grad PLUS loans, which are only limited by cost of attendance.

full price of attendance under a separate program called PLUS.[14] For example, an undergraduate attending a private college with a total yearly price tag of $50,000 (including living expenses) could borrow no more than $9,500 for the first year, but a graduate student could borrow the entire $50,000 with no questions asked. Graduate students pay higher interest rates than undergraduates: 5.8–6.8 percent for loans made during the 2015–16 academic year, depending on the amount borrowed.

Students generally begin repaying their loans six months after they leave college, either by graduating or dropping out, or after they reduce their enrollment intensity to less than half-time. The default repayment plan is for students to make monthly payments for ten years. At current interest rates, undergraduate borrowers on the ten-year repayment plan can expect to pay about $103 per month for every $10,000 borrowed ($110–$115 for graduate students).[15]

The default repayment plan is not the only repayment plan available. Students can consolidate their federal loans into a single loan and choose a repayment term based on their total student indebtedness (including private loans). For example, borrowers with between $20,000 and $40,000 in student debt can repay their federal loans over up to 20 years instead of the standard 10.[16] For a borrower who left college carrying $30,000 in debt, monthly payments on the 20-year plan would be $186, as compared to $308 on the standard ten-year plan.

Under the Department of Education's bureaucratic jargon, these longer terms for consolidation loans are still part of the "standard repayment plan." But there is a panoply of other plans: the extended plan, graduated plan, and an alphabet soup of income-driven repayment plans including the income-based repayment plan, pay as you earn plan, income-contingent repayment plan, and income-sensitive plan.[17] Additionally, students can delay making any payments under a wide range of situations by applying for deferment or forbearance.[18]

Individually, each of these repayment options may be useful to borrowers in a given set of circumstances. In particular, income-driven plans represent an important safety net for borrowers, as they provide protection from unaffordable monthly payments and forgive remaining balances after a set period of time. But collectively, they create a repayment system that is complicated and confusing at best and, at worst, disastrous for borrowers who fail to navigate it successfully.

LOANS TO PARENTS AND PRIVATE STUDENT LOANS

In almost all cases, students who want to borrow to pay for college should maximize their federal borrowing before going anywhere else. The interest rates offered by the federal government are usually well below what is offered in the private market, and the flexible repayment plans available for federal loans, such as income-driven repayment, and other safety nets such as deferment, forbearance, and forgiveness, are rarely available in the private sector. Parents who want to borrow money to pay for their children's education will likely be better off having their children borrow the money and then helping them pay it back later. Some parents may be able to borrow on better terms using their home equity, but this option is not available to many low- and middle-income families.[19]

But what options do families have once they have exhausted the federal borrowing limits for undergraduate students, such as the $5,500 limit for first-year dependent students? They have two main choices: borrow more from the federal government under a parent lending program or borrow from private banks. Both of these options are risky for the family because most of these loans charge relatively high interest rates and do not allow for repayment based on the borrower's income.

Federal lending to parents occurs through the Parent Loan for Undergraduate Students (PLUS) program, which was created in 1980. This is the same PLUS program that has also made loans to graduate students since 2005. PLUS has changed over the years from a limited program aimed at relatively affluent families who sent their children to expensive private colleges to one that provides unlimited borrowing (up to the price charged by the college) to a relatively broad group of families at a wider range of institutions, including public and for-profit colleges.[20]

PLUS loans are made to parents regardless of their ability to repay the loan. Parents do have to pass a credit history check, but they are only denied access to a PLUS loan if they are significantly delinquent on previous loans or have other adverse elements in their credit history.[21] In other words, a family that makes $30,000 per year but has never been in financial trouble (perhaps because they have never taken a loan) can borrow $40,000 a year to send a child to an expensive college. This example is extreme, but federal data indicate that low-income parents sometimes borrow PLUS loans.[22] These parent loans open the gates to colleges that students would otherwise be unable to afford, but put parents in the unenviable position of having to choose between taking on debt they are going to struggle to repay and telling their children to look elsewhere for college.

Parent PLUS loans totaled $10.3 billion in 2013–14, and were particularly common at private colleges. Parents of students at private, non-profit colleges make up 32 percent of PLUS borrowers, despite accounting for only 16 percent of enrollment. Parents of students at for-profit colleges are similarly overrepresented: 17 percent of borrowers vs. 10 percent of enrollment. Parents of students at public colleges are less likely to borrow PLUS loans, but still represent nearly half of PLUS borrowers since 77 percent of students are enrolled in this sector.[23]

Parents also use a variety of other ways to pay for their children's college educations, ranging from working more to borrowing against their home equity or retirement account (if they have one) to borrowing from other relatives or private banks. The broader issues of how parents pay for college is beyond the scope of this book, but private loans merit a brief discussion because students use them as well.

Private student loans are made by a variety of companies, so comprehensive data on the entire market are even sparser than for federal loans. However, a few key facts are clear from data assembled by both the federal government's Consumer Financial Protection Bureau (CFPB) and a consortium of private lenders.[24] First, private loans account for a relatively small portion of total outstanding debt: 7.5 percent, or $91.8 billion, according to the industry group. Second, the volume of new private loans grew rapidly during the run-up to the financial crisis, but fell sharply after that. According to the CFPB, the private loan market grew from less than $5 billion in 2001 to more than $20 billion in 2008, then fell to less than $6 billion in 2011. Third, both the industry consortium and the CFPB report that more than 90 percent of private student loans now require a co-signer, which makes the loans less risky for the lenders by making another party jointly responsible for the loan but also makes the loans harder to get.

Perhaps the most important difference for borrowers is that private loans generally do not allow students to repay based on their income. As a result, struggling borrowers can avoid delinquency and default by capping their federal payments based on their income, but often have to default if they are unable to make their private loan payments.[25] Student loans are not dischargeable in bankruptcy (except in rare circumstances), leaving struggling private borrowers with few options.

Private loans are most commonly used at private nonprofit and for-profit colleges. Twelve percent of undergraduates at these colleges took out private loans in 2011–12, as compared to 7 percent at public four-year colleges. Private lending to students who have weak repayment prospects, such as many of those enrolled at for-profit colleges, is particularly troubling. Graduate students are somewhat less likely to take on private loans, probably because they have unlimited access to PLUS loans.[26] Unfortunately, high-quality evidence on private borrowing is hard to come by because these loans are made by private entities that do not publish detailed data.

Now that we have dispensed with describing the complicated set of financing options available to college students and their families, we can turn to the main subject of this chapter: how much do student borrow?

HOW MUCH DO STUDENTS BORROW?

How much students borrow and whether they will be able to repay their loans are just two of the trillion-dollar questions that are difficult to answer accurately as a result of inadequate data from the U.S. government. University of Michigan economist Susan Dynarski illustrated this situation with a provocative analogy:

> Imagine that a big, complicated company holds a huge portfolio of loans, many of which are in default or delinquency. The company's leadership and some vocal shareholders demand a detailed review but receive a thin and incomplete report from the loan division.
>
> Financial analysts at headquarters want to scrutinize the data. But the loan division doesn't turn it over. Without better data, the firm can't move forward.
>
> This dysfunctional enterprise is fictional, but in at least some respects it bears more than a passing resemblance to the United States government, which has a portfolio of roughly $1 trillion in student loans … The Education Department, which oversees the portfolio, is playing the part of the loan division—neither analyzing the portfolio adequately nor allowing other agencies to do so.[27]

The U.S. Department of Education should be able to provide current, comprehensive information on the 90 percent of the student lending market that it controls given that it maintains records on all federal borrowers and their repayment histories. But the Department of Education only makes available very limited information on federal debt overall. For example, since 2013 it has published the number of borrowers in various repayment plans but the data do not include any details such as whether students who enter an income-based repayment plan renew their eligibility.[28] It also publishes some information broken down by institution, such as the number and amount of loans made and default rates. In order to understand the scope of the repayment challenges currently facing borrowers, we'd need to see data that would reveal information on repayment behavior across time.

The best data on federal student lending come not from the education department, but from the U.S. Department of the Treasury. Treasury researchers recently released information based on a nationally representative group of borrowers whose loan records were linked to income data held by the Internal Revenue Service.[29] In a single report, the Department of the Treasury made public more information about student loan repayment than the lender itself has provided in its entire history. However, it is unclear if this type of data release will be a regular event or if it was simply a one-time effort.

In the absence of comprehensive, periodic data releases from the public agency that makes the loans, policymaking and research have been based on a variety of datasets assembled by both the federal government and private entities.[30] Aggregate, institution-level data are collected by the U.S. Department of Education as well as private organizations such as the College Board. The Federal Reserve Bank of New York publishes information from its Consumer Credit Panel, a dataset drawn from records on individual borrowers maintained by the credit reporting agency Equifax.

The federal government also collects nationally representative data on a regular but infrequent basis through the U.S. Department of Education's National Postsecondary Student Aid Study (NPSAS), which is administered every four years. A limited number of additional studies follow selected students in the NPSAS data over time, both through college and after college. The Federal Reserve Board administers its Survey of Consumer Finances (SCF) every three years to a representative group of households.

The statistics reported in this chapter are based largely on the NPSAS, which is the only publicly available source of detailed information on borrowing at the student level, and the SCF, which is the only dataset that links information on outstanding debt and income and is administered on a regular basis. These datasets are not without limitations, but they are the best available in the absence of the information that the federal government ought to be providing.

Again, no student is typical, but how much debt does the average student take on to pay for college? This is a surprisingly hard question to answer precisely, but the most recent NPSAS, from 2011–12, is the best place to look.[31] NPSAS collects information on borrowing from students through a survey and by pulling their records from the federal government's loan database. The NPSAS data on federal loans are thus very accurate, but information on other types of loans (and total borrowing) relies on students to provide accurate information.

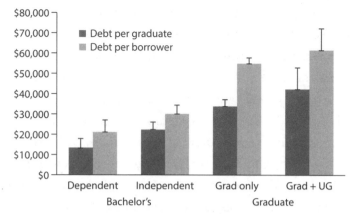

Figure 2.2. Mean debt levels, degree recipients, 2011–12
Source: Authors' calculations from NPSAS 2011–12. *Notes:* 2014 dollars.
Main bars show federal borrowing. Error bars show estimated nonfederal
borrowing.

Unfortunately, there is strong evidence that most students do
not have an accurate understanding of how much debt they
have.[32] NPSAS likely overstates average total borrowing because of how it incorporates information from student self-
reports.[33]

We report mean total borrowing for undergraduate and
graduate degree recipients in figure 2.2. We focus on federal
borrowing since it is measured most accurately, but also include a bar showing the estimate of total borrowing from
NPSAS. A comparison of the federal and total borrowing statistics shows how these data likely overestimate total borrowing. For example, the leftmost bar shows average federal borrowing per dependent bachelor's degree recipient of $13,368,
but average total borrowing of $18,038. This implies that fed-
eral borrowing is 74 percent of total borrowing, when we know

from aggregate data sources that it is closer to 90 percent. As a result, we focus on the federal numbers but provide the total estimates for reference.

Among bachelor's degree recipients, independent students borrow substantially more than dependent students, as we would expect since independent students are less able to draw on family resources and face higher loan limits in the federal lending programs. The average independent student graduates with about $22,000 in federal debt, compared to $13,000 for the average dependent student. Focusing only on students who borrow, average debt levels are about $30,000 for independents and $21,000 for dependent students. (These statistics, as well as median borrowing levels, are reported in appendix table 2.1.)

Graduate borrowing is a completely different ball game, as we might expect given the basically unlimited loans made available by the federal government. Graduate programs tend to be shorter than the four years or more it takes to earn a bachelor's degree, but graduate degree recipients still take on much more debt. The average graduate degree recipient takes on about $34,000 in federal debt for graduate school, leaving them with a total of $42,000 including their undergraduate debt. Excluding students who do not borrow, average debt per borrower is about $55,000 for graduate school and $61,000 including college.

These averages are just that—they don't tell us about the full distribution of borrowing. Figure 2.3 shows the full distribution of total borrowing for degree recipients in 2011–12. We are interested in part in seeing whether there are many

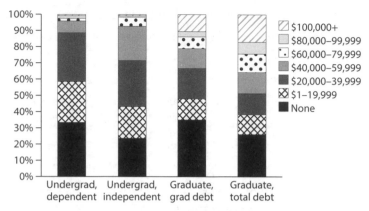

Figure 2.3. Distribution of total borrowing, degree recipients, 2011–12
Source: Authors' calculations from NPSAS 2011–12. *Notes:* 2014 dollars.

students with very large balances, so we use total borrowing (despite the data limitations described above) to make sure we do not miss anyone in this situation, while acknowledging that we may exaggerate the number of such borrowers as a result. Even using this generous definition, large balances among undergraduates are very rare. Most undergraduates leave college with less than $40,000 in debt (89 percent and 71 percent of dependents and independents, respectively). The aspiring environmentalist with $90,000 in debt is fairly lonely in the top 1 percent of borrowers.[34]

Once again, the data show why graduate students need to be in a category of their own. Including their undergraduate debt, nearly one-quarter accumulate more than $80,000 in debt, and 17 percent take on more than $100,000. Nearly half of graduate degree recipients leave school with at least $60,000 in total accumulated debt.

These data also show substantial numbers of students on the other end of the borrowing spectrum. Among dependent undergraduates, one-third take on no debt at all and 58 percent leave college with less than $20,000 in debt. Almost a quarter of independent students do not borrow, with many more borrowing small amounts (one-fifth take on some debt but less than $20,000). Graduate students also vary widely in their borrowing behavior. A sizeable portion take on enormous debt loads, but more than a quarter leave school debt-free.

Focusing on degree recipients provides some context for media reports of deeply indebted college graduates living in their parents' basements, but ignores the students who never cross the finish line. Among students who start a four-year degree, only 58 percent earn a bachelor's degree from any institution within six years; at two-year colleges, completion rates (including associate and bachelor's degrees from any institutions) are a paltry 26 percent.[35] Students who leave college with debt but no degree are likely to find themselves in a particularly weak position to pay off their loans.

Figure 2.4 shows the average borrowing of first-year undergraduate students, continuing to focus on federal debt while also reporting estimated total debt. These are the debt amounts these students would have if they dropped out after one year, which of course would be higher for students who drop out after multiple years of enrollment (and recall that debt limits increase in the sophomore and junior years). These data are broken down by sector to show how average borrowing behavior varies at different types of institutions.[36]

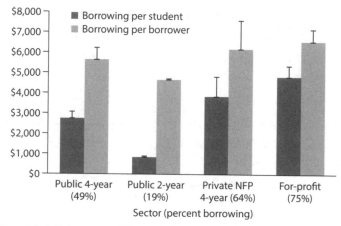

Figure 2.4. Borrowing of first-year students, 2011–12
Source: Authors' calculations from NPSAS 2011–12. *Notes:* 2014 dollars.
Main bars show federal borrowing. Error bars show estimated nonfederal
borrowing. Percent borrowing (federal or estimated nonfederal) appear in
parentheses.

How many students borrow at all varies across sector much
more than the average amount borrowed. The typical first-
year student borrower at a community college takes on $4,653
in federal loans, but less than one-fifth of students borrow at
all. Average debt levels among first-year borrowers at public
four-year colleges are somewhat higher ($5,640), but nearly
one-half of students borrow. As a result, average debt per
first-year student diverges markedly between the two sectors:
$845 at community colleges and $2,717 at public four-year
colleges.

Borrowing is much more common at private colleges, both
four-year non-profits and all for-profits. Most first-year students borrow, and the average borrower takes on more than
$6,000 in loans for their first year. NPSAS estimates of non-
federal borrowing are highest at four-year, private, non-profit

colleges, suggesting that students at these institutions are most likely to need to borrow more than the federal loan limits in order to pay the price of attendance.

All in all, the average one-year college dropout will leave school with a relatively small amount of debt. But, as we will show later, these turn out to be the students who struggle the most to stay on top of their loan payments. A big part of the explanation for this fact is that the strength of a borrower's financial position is determined by both his debt and his income. That's the subject to which we now turn.

HOW MUCH DO YOUNG HOUSEHOLDS OWE?

What is the financial burden of student loan debt on U.S. households? The first step to addressing this question is to look at how much Americans owe on their student loans, which is affected by the borrowing behavior of students over the past few decades, the payments they have made since leaving school, and patterns of household formation. We take a broad look at a group we call "young households," which are households where the adults have an average age of between 20 and 40, and also break this group down by education given the stark differences in borrowing behavior among dropouts, college graduates, and graduate degree holders.

Thirty-eight percent of all young households have at least some education debt, as shown in table 2.2. The average household with debt has an outstanding balance of approximately $31,000. Among households that are making payments on their loans, the average monthly payment is $276, or 7 percent

Table 2.2. **Outstanding Debt, Households Aged 20–40, 2013**

	All Households	Maximum Education of HH		
		Some College	Bachelor's	Graduate
Percentage of households with debt	38%	44%	52%	54%
Households with debt				
Debt per adult in household	$20,998	$13,871	$21,835	$35,426
Total debt	$31,063	$18,431	$30,198	$59,537
Wage income	$53,546	$34,688	$54,284	$93,301
Households making monthly payments				
Monthly payment	$276	$170	$262	$450
Payment-to-income ratio	7%	8%	7%	6%

Source: Authors' calculations from 2013 Survey of Consumer Finances.
Notes: All amounts in 2014 dollars. Payment-to-income ratio based on wage income. Payment data exclude households with reported monthly payments larger than reported monthly income. "All Households" include those with no college education.

of income. Large debt loads bring up these averages, so median debt loads and payments are lower: $193 per month, which translates to 4 percent of monthly income (appendix table 2.2).

Is a $276 monthly student loan payment affordable for the typical household? Of course, it depends on the household's specific circumstances, but information on other spending categories provides useful context. Figure 2.5 shows that the aver-

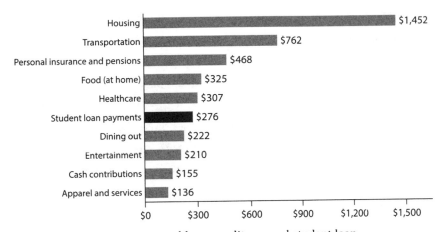

Figure 2.5. Average monthly expenditures and student loan payments, 2013
Source: 2013 Survey of Consumer Finances and 2013 Consumer Expenditure Survey. *Notes:* 2014 dollars.

age monthly payment of $276 is within the ballpark of what the average household spends on entertainment ($210), dining out ($222), and healthcare ($307), and much less than big-ticket items such as housing ($1,452) and transportation ($762).

More educated households have a lot more education debt, as we would expect given the patterns in borrowing documented above. The average household with debt where at least one member has a graduate degree has nearly $60,000 outstanding, compared to less than $20,000 for households with some college experience but no four-year degrees. The naïve interpretation that $60,000 is three times worse than $20,000 is rendered obviously wrong by looking at income data. The households with a graduate degree make more than $100,000 on average, compared to less than $40,000 for the households with some college but no degree (appendix table 2.2). And larger debts are generally paid off over longer periods of time.

These debt loads and income levels translate into average monthly payments that are lower as a percentage of income for the affluent, high-debt, highly educated households than for the lower debt, less-educated households. These data make clear that looking at debt levels without considering income is essentially useless and often misleading. This is one of the major themes of this book, and one that we will return to in later chapters to examine subjects such as how the financial well-being of borrowers has changed over time and the likely impacts of broad-based policies such as interest-rate reductions.

***

We don't know as much as we need to about the market for student loans in the United States, but several key facts are clear from the available evidence. First, the market is far from monolithic, with the enormous balances that dominate the popular press largely due to the debt of students who earn graduate and professional degrees. Balances in excess of $100,000 are not uncommon among this group, but among bachelor's degree holders, total borrowing of less than $40,000 is the norm and anything more than $60,000 is largely unheard of.

Second, these patterns of borrowing largely correspond to the borrowing policies set by the federal government. Graduate students can borrow as much as they want to, and they do. Independent undergraduates can borrow more than dependent students, and they do. Parents can borrow money even if they are unlikely to be able to repay it, and some do.

Third, the average household is not drowning in student loan debt. Monthly payments on education loans average $276, about 7 percent of the household's monthly income and a bit more than what it spends on dining out. The majority of households devote 4 percent or less of their income to making payments.

Finally, and most importantly, what matters is not the level of debt but the borrower's ability to repay it. The data show that graduate degrees are associated with huge balances, but also higher incomes. Put another way, the richest 20 percent of young households held 31 percent of all outstanding education debt in 2013.[37] Looking more broadly at all households age 20 and above, the top fifth in terms of income held 44 percent of all education debt.

In chapter 4 we will return to the subject of which borrowers are truly struggling and we will discuss how to help them in later chapters, but first we take a step back to document how we got where we are.

Appendix Table 2.1. **Cumulative Borrowing, Degree Recipients**

| | Bachelor's | | Graduate | |
	Dependent	Independent	Grad Only	Grad + Undergrad
Federal Borrowing				
Debt per graduate				
Mean	$13,368	$22,412	$33,626	$42,207
Median	$10,418	$21,971	$17,710	$26,804
Debt per borrower				
Mean	$21,252	$29,951	$54,685	$61,249
Median	$22,035	$28,703	$38,797	$47,938
Total Borrowing				
Debt per graduate				
Mean	$18,038	$26,248	$37,301	$52,845
Median	$13,959	$25,002	$21,356	$37,503
Debt per borrower				
Mean	$27,223	$34,428	$57,614	$71,913
Median	$25,002	$32,555	$41,670	$58,297

Source: Authors' calculations from NPSAS 2011–12.
Note: All amounts are in 2014 dollars.

Appendix Table 2.2. **Outstanding Debt, Households Aged 20–40, 2013**

	All Households	Maximum Education of HH		
		Some College	Bachelor's	Graduate
Percentage of households with debt	38%	44%	52%	54%
Mean debt per person, all households	$8,015	$6,139	$11,382	$19,175
Households with debt				
Mean debt per person	$20,998	$13,871	$21,835	$35,426
Median debt per person	$11,280	$7,622	$13,974	$25,406
Mean total debt	$31,063	$18,431	$30,198	$59,537
Median total debt	$17,480	$12,805	$19,309	$40,650
Mean wage income	$53,546	$34,688	$54,284	$93,301
Median wage income	$40,650	$27,439	$47,764	$78,252
Mean total income	$61,858	$41,146	$60,159	$108,714
Median total income	$45,732	$31,504	$49,797	$84,349
Households making monthly payments				
Mean monthly payment	$276	$170	$262	$450
Median monthly payment	$193	$102	$203	$325
Mean payment-to-income ratio	7%	8%	7%	6%
Median payment-to-income ratio	4%	3%	5%	4%

Source: Authors' calculations from 2013 Survey of Consumer Finances.
Notes: All amounts are in 2014 dollars. Payment-to-income ratio based on wage income. Payment data exclude households with reported monthly payments larger than reported monthly income. "All Households" include those with no college education.

How Did We Get Here?

Student debt has exploded over the last two decades by almost every measure. The $1.3 trillion in student debt owed by Americans is more than triple what it was just ten years ago (figure 1.1). The run-up in outstanding debt reflects three principal facts: more Americans are going to college (and obtaining higher degrees), more students are borrowing for college, and student borrowers are taking on larger amounts of debt.

Over the last 20 years, the share of Americans in their late twenties who had attended college at some point increased from 53 percent to 63 percent; the share with at least a bachelor's degree increased from 24 to 34 percent.[1] Over this period, the share of undergraduate students taking out loans more than doubled, from 19 percent to 43 percent, and the average amount borrowed (per year) by those taking out loans increased from $6,300 to $7,400 (in 2014 dollars).[2] The combination of these upward trends in educational attainment and borrowing levels nearly doubled the share of U.S. households age 20–40 with education debt, from 20 percent to 38 percent. Among households with debt, the average outstanding debt per adult increased from $8,300 to $21,000.[3]

Why are more students borrowing and why are they borrowing more? The increase in borrowing since the creation of the first major federal student loan program in the 1960s reflects the interaction of a series of policy choices with rising college prices and changes in the broader economy. Federal lawmakers have made debt available to a broader group of students over a time period when colleges were raising their prices. Put simply, there's more debt because more Americans have a need to borrow and because the federal government will lend to more of them without asking any questions. This chapter explains the societal and policy changes that have gotten us where we are today.

MORE STUDENTS, MORE BORROWERS, MORE DEBT

The public discussion of student loans often focuses on total outstanding debt, with the crossing of the $1 trillion mark attracting much notice. But much of this discussion misses the fact that rising outstanding debt in part reflects rising educational attainment. As more Americans go to college and complete higher degrees, we would expect total debt to rise. Indeed, we would view this increase in a positive light to the extent that these students are making good investments in their futures.

Figure 3.1 shows the rise in postsecondary enrollment relative to its 1967 level of 5.5 million full-time equivalent students (including both undergraduate and graduate students).

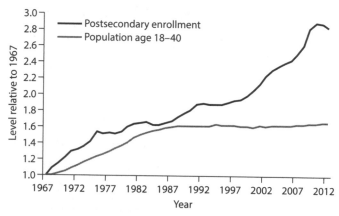

Figure 3.1. Full-time equivalent postsecondary enrollment and U.S. population aged 18–40, 1967–2012
Source: Digest of Education Statistics 2013 (Table 307.10) and authors' calculations from October Current Population Survey. Base numbers (1967) are 5.5 million for enrollment and 57 million for population aged 18–40.

Enrollment increased in fits and starts in the succeeding years to its current level of more than 15 million students. This increase partly reflected population growth in the 1970s and early 1980s, but by the mid-1980s the U.S. population aged 18–40 (roughly the age group from which most students are drawn) had plateaued. Enrollment growth was particularly dramatic beginning around the year 2000 through the middle of the Great Recession.

This growth in enrollment coincides with the large recent increases in student loan debt. Total annual borrowing more than doubled from $54 billion in 2000 to its peak of $124 billion in 2010 before receding to the most recent estimate of $108 billion. But figure 3.2 also shows earlier periods of relatively rapid increases, particularly in the late 1970s and mid-1990s. The dominant source of student loans is the federal govern-

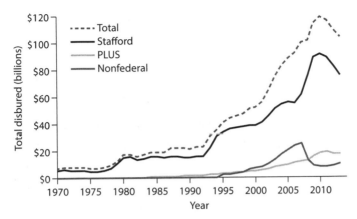

Figure 3.2. Student loans disbursed by year, 1970–2013 ($ Billions)
Source: College Board 2014 Trends in Student Aid and additional data from
Sandy Baum. *Notes:* 2014 dollars. Total loans also include other federal loans,
which totaled between $1 and $6 billion each year over this period.

ment's Stafford program, but the PLUS program for graduate
students and parents of undergraduates has experienced steady
growth, and nonfederal (mostly private) loans took off in the
2000s before collapsing during the economic crisis.

The fact that more students are going to college—and staying there longer—explains some of the growth in student loan
debt, but certainly not most of it. This is illustrated by a simple
calculation. In 1992, there were 10 million full-time equivalent students and $24 billion in loans, or about $2,300 in loans
per student. Twenty years later, when enrollment was 15.6 million, we would expect total loan volume of $36 billion if loans
per student had remained the same. But in fact total loan volume was $114 billion 2012. In other words, enrollment growth
alone explains roughly $12 billion, or 13 percent, of the $90
billion increase.[4]

We can run a more sophisticated version of this back-of-the-envelope calculation using household-level data from the Federal Reserve Board's Survey of Consumer Finances. The average debt of young households increased from less than $1,000 in 1989 to more than $7,000 in 2013. Among households with debt, average balances have increased from $5,800 to $19,300. But part of this increase is driven by rising levels of educational attainment—more people going to college at all, and those going more likely to complete undergraduate and graduate degrees. We calculate what average debt in 2013 would look like if educational attainment remained at its 1989 level. We find that increases in college attendance and attainment explain 30 percent of the increase in average debt over this period.[5]

The increase in student loans is a story of both demand and supply. Debt had only been able to increase insofar as someone, either the federal government or private lenders, was willing to make more dollars available to borrow. Through a series of policy changes, the supply of federal loans has been increasing steadily since the creation of the first major program in the 1960s.

UNCLE SAM OPENS THE MONEY SPIGOT

President Lyndon B. Johnson may be America's most famous student borrower, despite the fact that he attended college at a time when student borrowing was uncommon. By the time he graduated from Southwest Texas State Teachers' College in 1930, Johnson owed $220, equivalent to about $3,100 today.

And that was just what he borrowed from the college's loan fund. He used those dollars to support conspicuous consumption during his college years, and his spending habits ultimately led him to have to take a year off from school to work full-time in order to make ends meet. Johnson's troubles with debt were not limited to the loans his college gave him. He also had at least one private student loan, as well as an auto loan that became delinquent, leading him to hide the car so that the lender could not repossess it.[6]

With that context, it might come as no surprise that it was President Johnson who created the Guaranteed Student Loan (GSL) program—later renamed the Stafford program. Understanding the need for a system of financial support for students, he signed the Higher Education Act into law in 1965. HEA had a broad, lasting impact on higher education, including the creation of the first federal grant program for college students, but Johnson was personally most interested in the loan program.[7] As a congressman, he proposed a policy on student loans that eventually became part of HEA.[8]

HEA was the genesis of the federal loan program that persists today, but it was not the first student loan program or even the first federal program. Some individual colleges created their own programs, but few created strong programs and encouraged students to take advantage of them.[9] There were also various other private initiatives. In the 1920s, a philanthropic foundation launched an ambitious experiment aimed at "making loans on business terms to college students, with character and group responsibility as the basis of credit, without the usual forms of commercial collateral."[10] In the 1950s, a group of corporate executives in Boston who were worried about rising college prices created a loan guarantee program that they believed would be a more cost-effective way to help students than a scholarship fund.[11]

The law that opened the door to federal student loans was the National Defense Education Act (NDEA), which in 1958 allowed colleges to loan federal money to students pursuing careers in teaching, science, math, engineering, and foreign languages.[12] This program, which was initially fueled by American fears of inferiority in the space race with the Soviet Union, receives no new federal dollars today but remains through the Perkins loans that colleges make to students.[13] NDEA also contained provisions that allowed students who became public school teachers to have their loans forgiven, an early precursor to the contemporary forgiveness policies we will discuss in later chapters.

The National Defense Student Loans may have opened the door to Johnson's broader Guaranteed Student Loan program, but HEA was forged in large part as a political compromise between the interests of low-income families (who got a new grant program) and middle- and upper-middle-income families (who got a new loan program).[14] This latter group of families would form an important constituency for federal student loans as these loans evolved from a means-tested program at their inception to a universal program today. What started as a policy aimed at middle-income families can still be thought of as such only if one has a very broad definition of "middle income."

The first experiment with universal student loans was brief. After the U.S. Congress removed all income limits with the passage of the Middle Income Student Assistance Act in late 1978, the cost of the program exploded, in part due to low interest rates offered by the government relative to the high market rates that prevailed at the time.[15] Republicans (including President Reagan) led a successful charge to re-impose income restrictions on student loans in 1981. The growth of student loans subsequently slowed, but only briefly.[16]

Federal student loans again became available to all college students regardless of their financial circumstances—this time permanently—when Congress created the unsubsidized loan program in 1992. Unlike the Guaranteed Student Loan program (which had been renamed the Stafford program in 1987), the new loans accumulated interest while the students were enrolled. At the same time that this new lending program expanded affluent students' access to student loans, it also included an increase in loan limits and the elimination of borrowing limits on federal loans available to parents (PLUS).[17]

Not surprisingly, this set of policy changes was followed by arguably the most rapid increase in student borrowing in history. Stafford loan borrowing had been stable at $1,500–$1,800 per student (in 2014 dollars) from 1980 through 1992, but then more than doubled within three years, to $3,400 in 1995. Figure 3.3 puts each of the key policy changes discussed in this section in the context of Stafford loan disbursement per (full-time equivalent) student. This is not a causal analysis, as clearly other factors are at play.[18] For example, the expansion of the PLUS program to include graduate students in 2005 surely led to additional borrowing in subsequent years, but the rapid increases in 2008 and 2009 likely had more to do

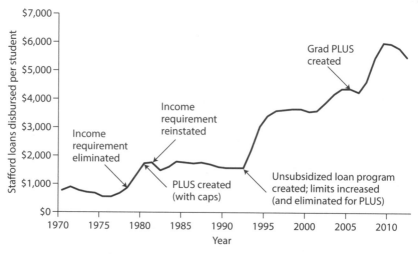

Figure 3.3. Stafford loan volume per full-time equivalent student and history of major changes to program, 1970–2012
Source: See Figures 3.1 and 3.2. *Notes:* 2014 dollars.

with the economic downturn. But the apparent relationship between loan volume and key policy changes such as the 1992 HEA amendments strongly suggest that these policy choices matter.

The transformation of loans from a nod to middle-class families to a universal entitlement allowed the federal government to increase aid to students (and colleges) at a much lower cost to taxpayers than the same dollars provided as grants would have cost. The reason is straightforward: a $1,000 grant costs taxpayers $1,000, whereas a $1,000 loan costs much less because the student is expected to pay it back. Figure 3.4 shows that loans surpassed grants as the dominant form of federal aid in 1981.[19] Even after the increase in the size of Pell grants in the early years of the Obama administration, the federal

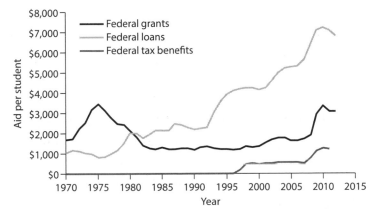

Figure 3.4. Federal spending on postsecondary aid programs per full-time equivalent student, 1970–2013
Source: College Board 2014 Trends in Student Aid and additional data from Sandy Baum. *Notes:* 2014 dollars.

government disbursed roughly twice the number of loan dollars as grant dollars. In the early 2000s, the ratio was closer to three to one.

Loans are not the only means through which federal support for higher education has shifted from an anti-poverty program created under President Johnson to one that reaches further up the income ladder. For every dollar it spends on Pell grants to low-income students, the federal government currently spends 55 cents on education tax benefits, which largely go to middle- and upper-middle-income students.[20]

Lawmakers resisted political pressure to create these tax benefits for many years. Johnson administration officials cited the original Guaranteed Student Loan plan as a way to appease relatively affluent voters who wanted tax credits for college expenses.[21] In 1978, income restrictions on federal loans were removed, at least partly in response to similar constituencies that were demanding the introduction of education tax credits.[22] Rising college prices have long concerned relatively affluent families (who tend to benefit most from tax credits).[23]

Rising college prices are the proverbial elephant in the room in any discussion of student loan debt. Students borrow more as colleges charge more, and some analysts worry that colleges charge more because students can borrow more. The next section explores how and why college costs have grown alongside student loan debt.

ROLE OF COLLEGE PRICES IN THE RUN-UP OF STUDENT DEBT

College prices have been increasing for almost as long as data on them have been collected, but the increases are not nearly as large as they first appear. This is because there is a large and growing difference between the "list price" that colleges officially charge and the "net price" that students actually pay. The difference between these two prices reflects the fact that institutions provide individual-specific discounts and that students receive grant aid from the state and federal governments as well as other private entities. In 1990, a majority (56 percent) of full-time students at four-year colleges paid the list price, but only 25 percent paid the full list price in 2012.[24]

Figure 3.5 shows the sharp contrast between skyrocketing list prices, especially at private four-year colleges, and more modest increases in average net prices.[25] After adjusting for inflation, average net price for one year at public four-year col-

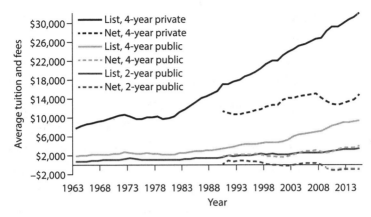

Figure 3.5. Average tuition and fees, 1963–2015
Source: 2013 Digest of Education Statistics Table 330.10 (1963–1989), College Board 2015 Trends in College Pricing (1990–2015). *Notes:* 2014 dollars.

leges has increased by about $2,100 since 1990. The increase at four-year private colleges was much larger (about $3,500), but average net price *decreased* by about $1,000 at community colleges (the negative net price shown in the figure means that the average student has money left over from grants to help cover living expenses). The historically low tuitions charged by many public four-year colleges mean that relatively small dollar increases represent large percentage increases—the $2,100 increase translates into a 111 percent increase from the 1990 level of $1,885.

The public perception that tuition inflation is rampant is not inconsistent with the reality of increasing net price, but it's probably inflated by the fact that people infer that students' net price is rising as rapidly as the sticker price. It's likely also driven by the fact that affluent families, who tend to be more politically vocal, are being asked to pay more, in some cases to keep tuition low for lower-income families. This scheme, in which colleges charge families based on their ability to pay, is often referred to as the "high-tuition, high-aid" model.

But the divergence between list and net price has occurred across the income spectrum because "aid" is not only awarded based on financial circumstances, but also on the college's desire to recruit particular students such as those with high SAT scores that will help the college's ranking. Several states also provide grant aid on the basis of academic achievement in high school.[26] The share of high-income families paying list price at private, four-year colleges dropped from 68 percent in 1989–90 to 23 percent in 2011–12. For low-income families, this statistic fell from 19 percent to 4 percent. There was a similar trend at public colleges, with the share of families paying list price falling from 89 percent to 59 percent for high-income families and from 35 percent to 4 percent for low-income families.[27]

Clearly, the increasing financial burden on students is likely to drive them to borrow more, but how much of the increase in borrowing that we've seen has been driven by the increased cost for students? On the flip side, how much of the increase is being driven by other factors? Brad Hershbein and Kevin Hollenbeck of the Upjohn Institute analyzed the borrowing patterns of bachelor's degree recipients between 1990 and 2012. They found that 15–20 percent of the increase in undergraduate debt over this period can be attributed to rising net prices, and posit that the unexplained increase likely reflects policy changes such as the advent of unsubsidized loans and also captures changes in student behaviors surrounding debt.[28]

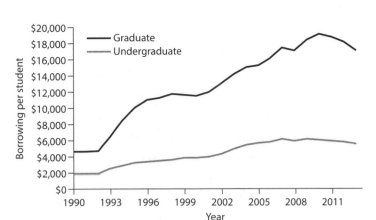

Figure 3.6. Total borrowing per full-time equivalent student, 1990–2013
Source: College Board 2014 Trends in Student Aid. *Notes:* 2014 dollars.

The increases in undergraduate borrowing pale in comparison to the increases among graduate students. Figure 3.6 shows that borrowing per undergraduate student has increased by about $3,600 since 1990 (after adjusting for inflation), whereas graduate borrowing has increased by more than $12,000 per student. In the previous chapter, we showed how the market for student debt is extremely diverse, with the story changing depending on the segment of the market. The same is true for how this market has changed over time. Undergraduates are certainly borrowing more than they did in previous generations, but the largest debt increases have tended to accumulate among graduate students.

These divergent trends likely reflect larger increases in prices paid by graduate students. Average list price (tuition and fees) for graduate students increased by $7,700 between 1992 and 2012, compared to $5,100 for undergraduates over the same period.[29] However, these data understate the difference between the two sectors to the extent that grant aid for undergraduates increased at a faster rate than it did for graduate students. The limited available evidence suggests that this was the case, as list and net prices diverged more for undergraduate students than for graduate students.[30]

In addition to these differences across sectors, there is also important variation in prices and borrowing (and how they've changed over time) across institutions. List price at public four-year colleges (tuition and fees for in-state students) varied from $4,646 in Wyoming to $14,712 in New Hampshire in 2014–15. Over the last five years, a handful of states such as Maine and Montana have barely increased their tuition at all (above inflation), some have made modest increases, and some have made large increases. Arizona tops the list in dollar terms, with a $3,147 increase (43 percent) over five years, but Louisiana had the largest increase in percentage terms, at 54 percent ($2,576).[31] Of course looking at list prices may miss important changes in institutional practices that produce different patterns in net prices, but they clearly illustrate that families in different states face different pricing environments when it comes to sending their children to college.

WHY HAVE COLLEGE PRICES INCREASED?

College prices are an important determinant of borrowing levels, so understanding why prices have increased is key to understanding the increase in debt levels. A comprehensive examination of this question is beyond the scope of this book, but a brief review of the available evidence sheds some light on which explanations have the strongest support.

We have purposefully used the word price to describe what students and their families pay for college and graduate school (i.e., net price). We do this to distinguish it from the cost to the institution of educating its students. Price and cost are able to diverge when institutions charge different prices to different students, and when they have non-tuition revenue sources, such as private donations and, at public institutions, direct government support.

Price and cost often diverge but they are not entirely unrelated. Colleges sometimes raise prices in order to enable more spending that will expand the services they provide. And sometimes increases in the cost of doing business cause them to have to increase price. Unfortunately, even efforts to reduce the price that students pay out of pocket by providing them with grants and loans can have the unintended effect of raising prices. In 1930, MIT announced a loan program with the stated intention of using the additional funds to raise faculty salaries.[32]

Today's college representatives often bristle at the suggestion that they are increasing tuition to capture grants and loans, so it's worth pointing out how this can occur even if institutions aren't following this strategy explicitly. Simply put, it is easier for colleges to raise prices when students are shielded from the full cost of their education. Imagine that the government gave every American $100, which they had to spend on theater tickets. Theater owners would likely face an increase in demand for tickets, which would make it easier for them to raise prices. They probably would not see it as capturing the government subsidy, but would instead focus on all of the great programming and building upgrades made possible by the increased revenue.

Government subsidies should enable tuition increases in theory, but does it happen in practice? There is some high-quality evidence indicating that colleges respond to federal and state grant aid by raising their prices in some circumstances. One study found that institutions capture 12 percent of Pell grant aid, and another found that Georgia colleges captured up to 30 percent of state scholarship dollars.[33] A third study found that for-profit institutions eligible for federal aid charge 78 percent more than similar institutions that are not eligible.[34] But this effect may not hold for all forms of aid: a recent study found that federal tax benefits received by students did not impact tuition.[35] This may be because tax benefits are less transparent to students and institutions than state and federal aid programs.

The impact of loan availability on college prices is much more ambiguous. In theory, a loan should have a much smaller impact on tuition than a grant because a loan is not free money in the way that a grant is. At the same time, it is plausible that loans make it easier for colleges to raise prices because with loans, more students will have the means to afford a higher price tag. The purpose of loans is to expand access to educational opportunities. The downside is that if they are successful in achieving this goal, they also increase demand for higher education which potentially drives up tuition prices.

There is little high-quality evidence on the impact of loan availability on college tuition. One recent study came to an intuitively plausible finding—that the availability of federal loans is less likely to lead to tuition increases than federal grants—but is subject to limitations of the data and methodology.[36] An important avenue for future research is to determine not just whether loan availability drives up prices but how policymakers can blunt any impact.

The distinction between price and cost is helpful for distinguishing between factors that potentially affect student borrowing by increasing price only or both cost and price. The leading explanations can be put into two general categories. The first is that declining state support of public universities has led to price increases without any change in costs. In other words, students are paying more for basically the same service because the government is paying less of the bill. This explanation obviously applies more directly to public institutions, but a version of it could also be applied to private institutions during periods when government aid such as Pell grants declined in value (in inflation-adjusted terms).

The second explanation is really a category of explanations for increases in costs. These include the ever-increasing cost of providing labor-intensive services,[37] the growth of administrative positions,[38] and the provision of fancy (non-academic) amenities to students such as lazy rivers and climbing walls.[39] As colleges have faced rising costs due to a combination of choices they have made (e.g., hiring more administrators) and factors beyond their control (e.g., broader changes that have increased labor costs), this theory posits that they have passed along those higher costs to students in the form of higher net prices (by increasing tuition or reducing grant aid).

There is compelling evidence supporting the first explanation, especially for recent years. States have provided roughly $7,000 in per-student funding for higher education over the last three years, the lowest level in the past 30 years.[40] Prior to the Great Recession, states spent more than $9,000 per student on higher education. Increasing net prices and declines in state support have appeared together in previous recessions as declining tax revenues put pressure on state budgets, and there is also evidence that states have cut higher education funding to deal with other rising costs, particularly from Medicaid.[41]

Price increases that result from state funding cuts are essentially transfers from students and their families (who pay more in tuition) to taxpayers (who pay less in taxes, or spend the funds on other things). States have taken widely varying approaches to how large of a subsidy to provide to public colleges. It should come as no surprise that the state with the highest list price (New Hampshire) has the lowest funding level, and the state with the lowest list price (Wyoming) has one of the highest funding levels.[42] The "right" level of state support depends on a variety of state-specific factors and policy goals, but the data make clear that many students are paying more for college so that states can avoid tax increases or other spending cuts.

The fact that states have reduced their support for public higher education is clear, but these changes have not necessarily coincided with increases in borrowing levels. Hershbein and Hollenbeck point out that state appropriations per student fell by about 15 percent between 2000 and 2004 and had not returned to their 2000 level by the start of the recession. They point out that "Despite these reductions (and concomitant tuition increases), debt of graduating students changed little, especially relative to the large increases over the 1990s."[43] In other words, the intersecting relationships between state appropriations, tuition, and borrowing levels are not as straightforward as they first seem.

Are rising costs also to blame for rising prices at public colleges? Spending data suggest that they are a part of the story, but a smaller one. Between 2001 and 2011, when state support per student fell by $2,800, costs increased by less than $1,000 per student at public four-year colleges (on top of inflation).[44] These increases are not trivial; in percentage terms, spending went up 6 percent at research universities, 3 percent at master's institutions, and 9 percent at bachelor's institutions.[45] And cost increases would likely have been larger were it not for the continuing shift away from full-time faculty toward much less expensive part-time instructors.[46] But the cost increases observed at four-year public colleges are significantly smaller than the 29 percent drop in state support over this period.

Private universities are a different story. In general they do not receive much direct support from state governments, so declining state funding is not an immediate issue for them.[47] At private research universities, spending increased dramatically over the last decade by more than $7,000 per student, an increase of 21 percent. Private nonprofit master's and bachelor's colleges saw smaller increases of $1,500 (10 percent) and $650 (3 percent), respectively.[48] The larger increase at research universities may disproportionately reflect spending increases on graduate students. But research universities also tend to be the elite, selective institutions that may be more prone to offering expensive amenities to compete for talented undergraduate students.

Tying these strands together, what do we know about the reasons for rising college prices? At public four-year institutions, students are paying more largely because taxpayers are paying less, but there have also been modest increases in average spending levels. At community colleges, colleges are spending less and students are paying less. In the private sector, research universities have dramatically increased their spending, whereas other institutions have seen smaller increases. And in both sectors, there is some limited evidence to suggest that the increased availability of government support has allowed colleges to raise their prices to capture some of that aid.

***

How did we get here? Debt levels have risen through a combination of increased college attendance and attainment in the United States, which in turn increased enrollment; policy decisions at the state level that increased tuitions at public colleges; and federal policies that have expanded student loans from a modest program to a universal entitlement. But there are likely behavioral explanations at play as well, with students borrowing more than their predecessors for reasons that are not quantifiable. One possibility is that the perceived increase in college costs due to rapidly rising list prices has increased students' willingness to borrow. Additionally, borrowing may beget borrowing as it becomes the social norm to borrow larger and larger amounts to pay for college and graduate school.

An additional factor that is difficult to measure is the fungibility of debt. Historically, households used multiple sources of credit to finance investment in higher education. For example, some parents borrowed from their home equity to help their children pay for college. As the availability of these alternative sources of financing has changed over time, the demand for loans explicitly marketed to finance educational investments has changed as well.

These changes have not occurred evenly across the board. Price and borrowing changes have varied widely across institutions, and graduate borrowing has accelerated more than undergraduate borrowing. This latter fact means that much of the increased debt has accrued to households with graduate degrees. Figure 3.7 shows how average balances among households with different amounts of education have evolved since 1989. Households with graduate degrees have seen increases of almost $25,000 in outstanding education debt, compared to $15,000 for those with bachelor's degrees and $9,000 for households with some college but no degree.

Competing explanations aside, the simple fact remains that debt loads have increased dramatically in less than a

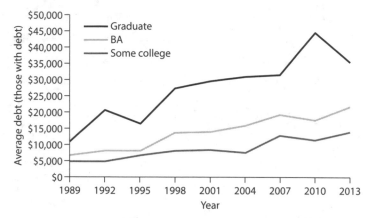

Figure 3.7. Average debt by educational attainment, 1989–2013
Source: Authors' calculations from Survey of Consumer Finances. *Notes:* Debt is calculated per adult in household. Sample is restricted to households aged 20–40 with education debt. 2014 dollars.

generation. Many more Americans have education debt, and they have much more of it. Do these increases in debt spell trouble for the borrowers, particularly those with the largest balances? Is the widely heralded "student loan crisis" just around the corner? That's the question to which we now turn.

4

Is a Crisis on the Horizon?

Federal regulators clearly have a lot to do to address
what amounts to a student loan crisis. (Total
student indebtedness is now about $1.2 trillion.)

—*New York Times* editorial, 2014[1]

The idea of a student lending crisis that is either already here
or just around the corner has become entrenched in the national dialogue about higher education, with headlines asking variations on the question "Will student loans be the next
mortgage crisis?"[2] This narrative alleges that college prices
and student debt levels are the latest bubble that will burst and
damage the broader economy, much as the collapse of the
housing market in 2007 led to a financial crisis and deep
recession.[3]

This narrative quickly withers in the face of even rudimen-
tary evidence on the student lending market in the United
States. Student loans are too small of a market and too iso-
lated from the private sector to cause anything close to the
kind of economic damage suggested by comparisons to the
housing crisis. Massive student loan defaults could make a
small dent in the federal budget, but they can't take down the
U.S. economy.

But could there be a different kind of broad-based student loan crisis, in which the typical borrower has made a poor investment and is saddled with payments for a degree that never paid off? This question is more difficult to answer. There are many disheartening examples of individuals with student debt who are facing difficult financial circumstances. Many of these borrowers are suffering the consequences of default or struggling to make payments for an education they regret pursuing. Of particular concern are borrowers who took on debt but never completed a degree. Since degree completion generally brings the largest economic rewards, these borrowers are often worse off than if they hadn't enrolled in the first place.

There are surely too many borrowers who are in crisis, but the available evidence runs counter to the popular narrative of a systemic student loan crisis. The economic return to a college degree is as high as it has been in a generation, and monthly payments remain manageable for the typical borrower. In this chapter, we explain why the large and rising volume of outstanding education debt needs to be interpreted not simply as a millstone around borrowers' necks but also in light of the educational investments it was used to finance.

WILL STUDENT LOANS TRIGGER THE NEXT FINANCIAL CRISIS?

It is easy to see parallels between the run-up in mortgage debt that preceded the financial crisis and the recent run-up in student loan debt. A 2008 Brookings Institution report provides a concise history of the housing market leading up to the financial crisis:

> A bubble formed in the housing markets as home prices across the country increased each year from the mid-1990s to 2006, moving out of line with fundamentals like household income. Like traditional asset price bubbles, expectations of future price increases developed and were a significant factor in inflating house prices ... The rapid rise of lending to subprime borrowers helped inflate the housing price bubble. Before 2000, subprime lending was virtually non-existent, but thereafter it took off exponentially.[4]

Housing prices stopped increasing in 2006 and began a sharp decline in 2007, leaving many homeowners owing more on the mortgage than their house was worth and the U.S. economy in the worst downturn since the Great Depression.

In both housing and education, individuals use debt to finance investments that will pay off over a long period of time in terms of both financial value and non-pecuniary benefits. Homeowners expect to accumulate more wealth than they would as renters, and college students expect to earn more after graduation than they would if they entered the labor market with only a high school diploma. In both cases, the loan serves as an instrument that allows the borrower to access an investment that they would not otherwise be able to afford. And in both cases, concerns arise about out-of-control prices and individuals taking out loans that they will ultimately struggle or fail to repay.

But what would need to occur for the student loan market to trigger a crisis like that seen in the mortgage market? Two conditions would need to be met. First, there would have to be a disconnect between the price of education and the value of education in the labor market, much as the housing market crash was driven by house prices failing to keep up with consumers' (and lenders') expectations. Leading up to the housing crisis, individuals were willing to pay high prices for their homes because they believed that the price accurately reflected the value of their investment. When the market adjusted, widely depressing home prices, many realized that the price they paid was far more than the value of their home and thus they were left with an underwater mortgage. A student borrower would find himself in a similar situation if he ultimately finds that the degree he has invested in doesn't provide the anticipated financial rewards. This would only occur at a macro level if tuition prices were generally out of line with value, such that the financial benefits do not outweigh the upfront costs including tuition, fees, and the earnings that students forgo when they are enrolled in school rather than working.

Second, the market for student loans would have to be large enough and sufficiently connected to the private sector to have ripple effects through the broader economy. The housing crisis led to a broader economic disaster because mortgages were packaged into financial products that were owned by banks and other financial institutions. The crash in housing prices hurt not just a large number of individual homeowners but also the financial institutions that owned their mortgages.[5]

Student loans have zero chance of becoming the next housing crisis because the market is too small and essentially functions as a government program rather than a market. The pool of outstanding student debt is large and growing, but only

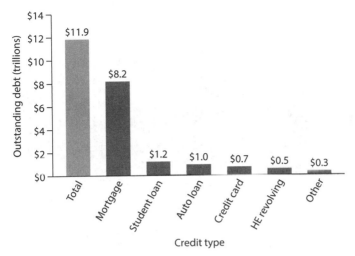

Figure 4.1. Outstanding debt, by type, 2015 ($ Trillions)
Source: Federal Reserve Bank of New York 2015 Q1 Report. *Notes:* Total
outstanding debt, in trillions of dollars, as of the first quarter of 2015. "HE
Revolving" is home equity revolving credit.

represents 10 percent of the overall credit market (figure 4.1).
In contrast, housing debt makes up nearly 70 percent of outstanding debt, reflecting the fact that households tend to hold
a large portion of their wealth in real estate. The increase in
housing debt is easily seen in figure 4.2, but the increase in
non-mortgage debt driven by student loans is barely notice-
able in the context of the broader picture of all types of debt.

This is not to say that student debt is not an important factor in the economy, but rather to show that it is unlikely that
even a complete collapse of this market would have the potential to upset the domestic economy to the same degree as
the collapse of the mortgage market. This is reinforced by the
fact that student loans are also held almost exclusively by the
federal government. Consequently, a broad-based crisis among

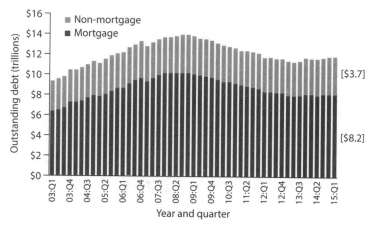

Figure 4.2. Outstanding household debt, 2004–15 ($ Trillions)
Source: Federal Reserve Bank of New York 2015 Q1 Report. *Notes:* 2014 dollars.

borrowers could put a dent in the federal budget, but would not lead to the failure of any significant financial institutions as occurred during the housing crisis.

IS THERE A SYSTEMIC CRISIS AMONG BORROWERS?

Student loans are not going to trigger the next economic crisis, but is there a systemic student loan crisis in the sense that a critical mass of borrowers made investments that won't pay off? This question is difficult to answer for two important reasons. First, we face the fundamental challenge of not being able to see into the future. In order to know with certainty whether an individual's education pays off in the long run, we'd need to be able to observe their entire lifetime of earnings. Naturally, the borrowers that hold most of the current pool of outstanding student debt are still in the middle of their working careers. We are thus left to rely on estimates of lifetime earnings, generally based on historical data, when trying to understand the long-run payoff of a postsecondary degree.

The second challenge is that it is difficult to measure the causal effect of education on earnings. In other words, even if we know how much money someone will make over the course of a lifetime, we have no way of knowing how much an individual would have made if he had obtained less education. As a result, we cannot observe the economic return to a college degree; we can only estimate it.

Many researchers have estimated the returns to education by comparing the earnings of individuals with different levels of education. The obstacle to doing this well is the difficulty of controlling for differences between individuals who attain different amounts of education. For example, if college graduates are more motivated than high school graduates and motivation is rewarded in the labor market, then a simple comparison of the earnings of these two groups will overstate the value of a college degree. Part of the difference in earnings will be due to the fact that the motivated college-educated workers would have earned more even if they had not gone to college.

How researchers address these challenges affects the results they get, but a large number of studies using a variety of methodologies have consistently found that the economic returns to college are positive and large. The Center on Education and the Workforce at Georgetown University used the relatively simple approach of comparing the earnings of workers with and without a college degree in a 2011 report.[6] The Georgetown researchers estimated that workers with a bachelor's degree earn 74 percent—or almost $1 million—more over the course of their lifetimes than workers without college degrees. This estimate doesn't take into account the fact that the college wage premium may be determined by factors other than the degree, but shows that there are large differences in earnings between workers with and without college degrees.

A more recent study calculated the rate of return on college degrees, taking into account basic worker characteristics such as age, race, and gender. Researchers at the Federal Reserve Bank of New York found that the rate of return on a bachelor's degree is 15 percent and has held steady at that level (a historic high) for the previous decade.[7] These estimates, which are reproduced in figure 4.3, take into account both the costs and the benefits of a college degree. This work suggests that the economic return on a college degree has not fallen, despite the growing cost of attendance and stagnant earnings. This counterintuitive result is driven in large part by the declining earnings among workers without college degrees. In other words, college-educated workers are paying more for college and not seeing significant increases in their earnings, but are avoiding the increasingly poor outcome of entering the labor market with only a high school diploma.

Research from the Brookings Institution has yielded similar conclusions.[8] In a study that factored in the cost of college, Michael Greenstone and Adam Looney showed that the increases in tuition that have been observed over the past few decades have been largely outweighed by simultaneous in-

Figure 4.3. Economic return on bachelor's and associate degrees, 1970–2013
Source: Jason R. Abel and Richard Deitz, "Do the Benefits of College Still Outweigh the Costs?" Federal Reserve Bank of New York *Current Issues in Economics and Finance* 20 no. 3 (2014), available at http://www.newyourfed .org/research/current_issues/ci20-3.html. Reprinted with permission.

creases in the financial reward of having a degree, such that the financial return of college is rising, despite the rising cost.

The returns on college may be growing even faster than suggested by the statistics in figure 4.3. The rate of return calculations ignore the fact that a steady or rising rate of return is being earned on an increasingly large investment. For example, $50,000 invested at a 15 percent rate of return would be worth $3.3 million after 30 years. But $75,000 invested at the same rate would be worth nearly $5 million. Commentators often lament the fact that students are paying a heftier price tag for college, but forget that this investment is earning a constant or growing rate of return.

The financial value of a college degree is not driven by heightened wages alone. Workers with degrees are also less

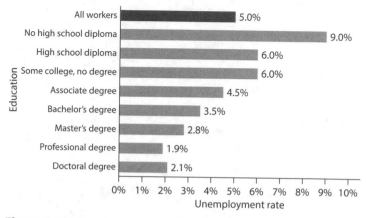

Figure 4.4. Unemployment rates by educational attainment, 2014
Source: "Earnings and unemployment rates by educational attainment," U.S. Bureau of Labor Statistics. *Notes:* Based on individual over age 25.

likely to be unemployed. Lower rates of unemployment further amplify the earnings advantage enjoyed by more educated workers. Data from the Bureau of Labor Statistics indicate that the rate of unemployment among individuals with bachelor's degrees was 3.5 percent in 2014, whereas the unemployment rate among Americans with only a high school diploma was 6 percent (figure 4.4). Individuals with graduate degrees have even lower unemployment rates, and those that never completed high school are the most likely to be unemployed.

The credibility of these relatively simple approaches to measuring the returns on higher education is bolstered by a number of more rigorous studies. These "quasi-experimental" studies exploit data on individuals who completed different levels of education for idiosyncratic reasons, and thus are unlikely to differ in unmeasured ways such as ability and motivation.[9] For example, University of Chicago economist Seth

Zimmerman found that students who just barely earned the grades needed for admission to a large public university in Florida were much more likely to attend any university than students who just missed the cutoff. These two groups of students were very similar in all respects, but those who gained admission earned 22 percent more as adults than those who did not.

All of the research measuring the financial return on a college degree has shortcomings. Studies that look at a broad group of workers cannot adequately account for the unmeasured differences of people who attain different levels of education, and studies that do account for those differences are generally focused on a very narrow group of individuals. But both types of work reach the same conclusion: the average financial return on a college degree is positive and large for the typical student.

Unfortunately, a positive return on average does not mean a positive return for everyone. Some students reap much higher than average benefits. Others earn significantly smaller benefits or even a negative return on their investment—that is, the benefits of their education don't exceed what they paid for it. An important dimension on which the returns to education vary is field of study. Recent work by the Hamilton Project at Brookings finds that average lifetime earnings vary by major from a low of $800,000 to a high of $2 million.[10] Naturally, there is even greater variation in earnings across individuals with the same major. The Hamilton Project report indicates that even the majors with the highest average earnings include individuals who do not earn very much.

Program of study is just one dimension along which the returns on a college degree vary systematically. There are a number of other factors that determine the return that students earn, including the quality of the institution they attend, their local labor market, and perhaps most importantly, whether or not they complete a degree. Research indicates that the returns on investment in higher education do not accrue uniformly as a student spends more time enrolled in school. Instead, the increase in earnings is concentrated at the time a student completes her degree.[11] This means that students who don't earn a degree are among the most likely to face a negative return on their investment. These students face the cost of enrollment, but may experience only a small fraction of the gains in earnings seen by individuals who cross the finish line.

The existence of distressed segments of a student lending market that is healthy overall is supported by a recent analysis of a remarkable new dataset assembled by the U.S. Department of the Treasury, which links data on federal borrowing to earnings records from tax returns for a nationally representative group of borrowers. The development of this dataset made it possible for analysts to examine the variation in outcomes across institutions in a more detailed way than was previously possible. Although it is difficult to effectively estimate the financial return at each institution, this Treasury study reveals some alarming trends in borrower well-being. Most notably, it finds that struggling borrowers are most likely to have attended certain types of institutions, particularly for-profit and community colleges. These borrowers earned far less than graduates from public and private, not-for-profit colleges, which likely explained why they were having less success in repaying their loans, despite small balances. But the study also noted that this dismal picture does not hold more generally:

> For most borrowers (and the majority of the student loan portfolio) the educations financed with their loans are associated with favorable economic outcomes, and borrowers are able to repay their debt even during recessionary periods.[12]

The fact that some students make educational investments that do not pay off is a crisis for them and an important broader problem that we will return to later in this book. More work needs to be done to identify the sources of subprime student loans, but the fact that these disheartening situations are not the norm means that there is no systemic crisis. Returns on investments in education remain positive, indicating that prices are not out of line with value and students are largely borrowing to finance investments that will pay off generously in the future.

ARE WE MOVING TOWARD A SYSTEMIC CRISIS?

The student loan market is not in crisis, but is such a crisis on the horizon? All of the available evidence suggests that most of today's borrowers are making investments that will pay off, but whether or not the market is headed for a crisis depends on whether these positive returns continue. The return on higher education could be eroded by an increase in the price of college or a decrease in the earnings of college-educated workers (relative to workers without a college degree). Price increases would only affect the return for future borrowers, but earnings decreases could affect current and previous borrowers as well.

The seemingly never-ending growth in college prices has attracted a great deal of attention, although the prices students actually pay have increased more slowly than the advertised sticker prices (see chapter 3). Undoubtedly students would prefer to pay less for college rather than more, and would likely borrow less if prices were lower. But for the purposes of assessing the health of the student loan market, growth in prices is not a problem on its own. Price increases only pose a threat to the ability of borrowers to repay their loans insofar as growth in the wage premium does not keep pace.

Without a crystal ball, it's difficult to say whether or not the growth in prices will begin to eat into the return on educational investments. On one hand, it's hard to imagine that growth in the relative earnings potential of college graduates will continue to keep pace with rising college prices, especially since much of the recent growth in the earnings premium has come from declines in the wages of non-college-educated workers. At the same time, the evidence presented in figure 4.3 shows that the economic return on college degrees increased and then remained high over a period when college prices were continuously rising.

A decline in the wage premium, independent of changes in tuition, could also cause future returns to depart from the historical trend. The wage premium reflects the fact that skilled workers, those with higher levels of education, are more productive than unskilled workers, but it is also influenced by a multitude of other factors, many of which are unrelated to the quality of the higher education system. For instance, an increase in the number of college-educated workers, without a corresponding increase in the number of jobs requiring a degree, may reduce the wage premium that these workers can command. Alternatively, increases in consumer demand for goods and services that are produced using highly skilled labor could increase the wage premium (by increasing competition by firms for educated workers). These types of changes are inherently difficult to predict but will play a critical role in shaping the market for student debt in the future.

One way to examine this issue further—without the aid of a crystal ball—is to examine how the earnings of student loan borrowers have evolved over time relative to borrowing. Figure 4.5 shows the mean and median wage income over time for the population of young households (aged 20–40) with education debt, along with the total amount of student loan debt borrowed. Over the last 20 years, growth in debt has far outpaced growth in annual earnings. Between 1992 and 2013, mean wage income grew by only $7,126 (in 2014 dollars), while mean borrowing increased by $23,211 (note that these figures reflect changes at the household rather than individual level).

Therefore, the increase in average education debt between 1992 and 2013 ($23,000) can be paid off with just a few years of the additional wage income ($7,000) that the average household is collecting each year.[13] An astute investor would gladly

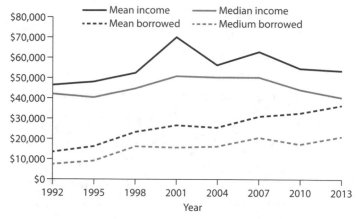

Figure 4.5. Mean and median income and borrowing among young households with education debt
Source: Authors' calculations using the Survey of Consumer Finances. *Note:* 2014 dollars. Based on households age 20–40 with outstanding student loan debt. Income is from wages and salaries only.

accept an additional $23,000 in debt in exchange for an extra $7,000 in annual income, since the investor would only get the debt once but would continue to receive the extra income every year. Examining total income, which includes business and investment income in addition to wages and salaries, shows the average borrower in an even stronger position given that this broader measure of income increased by $13,000 over this period (appendix table 4.1).[14]

Some analysts draw the opposite conclusion from the same data by noting that the average debt-to-income ratio has increased over time. We believe this approach is misleading because it compares the change in the "stock" of debt (total outstanding debt) to the change in the "flow" of income (annual earnings). The ratio of the stock of debt to the flow of income is not completely devoid of meaning. For a given level of annual income, borrowers would certainly prefer less debt. But what analysts and consumers should really care about is how an investment, like education, affects lifetime wealth. Increases in debt-to-income ratios do not necessarily constitute a reduction in lifetime wealth.

This fact is illustrated with a simple example, shown in table 4.1. Imagine an individual who has an opportunity to buy a rental property using a $50,000 loan. The investor expects to make a profit of $10,000 per year after taking into account maintenance, taxes, interest payments, and other costs. She currently has an income of $60,000 and existing debt of $10,000. Should she buy the rental property? Over 30 years, the increase in lifetime income will far exceed the $50,000 initial investment, to the tune of a $250,000 lifetime profit.[15] But looking at debt-to-income ratios suggests that the investor is worse off by making the investment. Debt as a percentage of annual income increases from 17 percent to 86 percent as a result of making what is clearly a good investment.[16]

Popular discussions about student debt often make a similar mistake of not properly comparing costs and benefits, or

Table 4.1. **Hypothetical Investment Example**

	Do Not Buy Property	*Buy Rental Property*
Total debt	$10,000	$60,000
Annual income	$60,000	$70,000
Debt-to-annual-income ratio	17%	86%
Lifetime income (over 30 years)	$1,800,000	$2,100,000
Lifetime wealth (lifetime income minus total debt)	$1,790,000	$2,040,000

not even considering benefits at all. When outstanding debt passed the $1 trillion mark it made headlines, but much less noted were the increases in economic activity that the underlying investments in education will likely produce over the next several decades.

Properly comparing the costs and benefits of an investment requires a long-term view, but that does not mean that short-term considerations are unimportant. In the stylized example shown in table 4.1, if the loan had to be paid off in a single year, the investment would not be possible even though it made financial sense in the long run. Making $50,000 in loan payments (plus interest) over the course of a year is unlikely to be feasible for someone with $70,000 in income.

The idea of education as a long-term investment is potentially at odds with the practical consideration of having to pay off education debts in a relatively short period. The standard repayment plan has borrowers making flat monthly payments for ten years. Although borrowers can stretch payments over longer periods of time (see chapter 2), for many borrowers the period over which the educational investment pays off does not match the period when they are expected to repay their debt. Even if the fundamentals of the investment were sound, this mismatch could cause borrowers to struggle to make their payments. If this occurs, student loans have failed at one of their primary aims: enabling borrowers to transfer wealth across stages of their life.

The large increases in debt loads over the last two decades could create repayment challenges for borrowers, especially those who use the default ten-year plan. We examine whether the month-to-month burden of student loan debt has grown

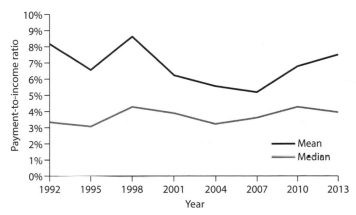

Figure 4.6. Monthly payment to income ratios for young households making payments on student loans, 1993–2013
Notes: Based on households aged 20–40 with education debt and positive monthly payments. Income is from wages and salaries only. Observations where monthly payment is more than monthly income are excluded.

over time by calculating the ratio of monthly payments made on education loans to monthly income for young households with outstanding student loan balances.

Figure 4.6 illustrates the surprising fact that the monthly burden of student loan repayment has not increased for the typical borrower over the last 20 years. The median monthly payment has remained essentially flat at 3 percent and 4 percent of monthly earnings in every year from 1992 through 2013. Mean monthly payments have been somewhat more variable, ranging from 5 percent to 8 percent, but have exhibited a similar overall pattern.[17] This analysis calculates payments as a share of wage income, but we find similar results using total income.[18]

We have focused on the mean and median payment-to-income ratios, but the incidence of very high debt burdens is also no more common than it was 20 years ago. For example, 7 percent of households in 2013 made student loan payments that consumed more than a fifth of their income, compared to 7–11 percent of households in the 1990s.[19] Payment ratios have also held steady for households at different levels of educational attainment. A likely explanation for why payment-to-income ratios have stayed the same while debt levels have increased is that the average repayment period of education loans increased over this period, from 7.5 years in 1992 to 12.5 years in 2013.[20]

The default rate is a commonly used indicator of borrower well-being that focuses on the worst outcome a borrower can face. The cohort default rate published annually by the U.S. Department of Education measures the percentage of borrowers who defaulted during the first three years after they entered repayment (default is currently defined as not making any payments for 270 days). The most recent default rate indicates that 12 percent of borrowers who entered repayment in 2012 defaulted within three years, a modest decrease from the prior year.[21]

Official three-year rates have only been reported for the last few years, but figure 4.7 shows two-, three-, and five-year rates calculated by the U.S. Department of the Treasury going back to 1970.[22] These data show the recent increase in default rates during and after the Great Recession, but also indicate that the highest levels of default occurred in the late eighties and early nineties, with five-year default rates as high as 41 percent. These trends are consistent with the notion that the rate of default increases during economic recessions and decreases

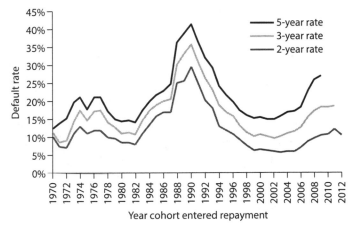

Figure 4.7. Default rates on student loans, 1970–2012 repayment cohorts
Source: Replication of official cohort default rate measure reported in data appendix of Adam Looney and Constantine Yannelis.

during periods of economic growth. This is likely driven by changes in both wages and unemployment.

Much of the public narrative around student debt would have you believe that the system of student lending is engulfed in crisis. It is true that many borrowers are facing personal crises related to student debt, but the overall body of evidence contradicts the notion that a student lending crisis exists on a systemic level. This distinction may seem semantic, but recognizing the difference has important implications for policy-making. The popular notion of a singular student loan crisis is an unfortunate distraction from efforts to address the undeniable fact that many borrowers are facing serious economic hardship that won't be alleviated by solutions designed to relieve a systemic crisis.

Appendix Table 4.1. **Borrowing and Income, Households with Education Debt**

Year	Amount Borrowed		Wage Income		Total Income	
	Mean Borrowed	Median Borrowed	Mean Income	Median Income	Mean Income	Median Income
1992	$13,258	$7,256	$46,420	$42,185	$48,774	$42,185
1995	$15,970	$9,321	$47,974	$40,389	$51,343	$46,603
1998	$23,325	$16,267	$52,617	$45,025	$55,190	$46,477
2001	$26,673	$15,774	$69,852	$50,798	$74,866	$52,134
2004	$25,701	$16,293	$56,560	$50,131	$62,795	$52,638
2007	$30,992	$20,552	$62,799	$50,239	$68,529	$54,806
2010	$32,743	$17,371	$54,467	$44,514	$61,738	$49,942
2013	$36,369	$21,341	$53,546	$40,650	$61,858	$45,732
Change, 1992–2013	$23,111	$14,086	$7,126	−$1,535	$13,084	$3,547

Note: All amounts are in 2014 dollars.

How Are Student Loans Impacting Borrowers and the Economy?

> Consider Shane Gill, a 33-year-old high-school
> teacher in New York City. He does not have a car.
> He does not own a home. He is not married ... like
> hundreds of thousands of others in his generation,
> he has put off such major purchases or decisions in
> part because of his debts ... That investment in his
> future has led to a secure job with decent pay and
> good benefits. But it has left him with tremendous
> financial constraints, as he faces chipping away at
> the debt for years on end.[1]

Student loan debt has been blamed for nearly all that ails the
U.S. economy, including depressed home ownership, lower
rates of entrepreneurship, and even the sluggish recovery from
the Great Recession.[2] The idea is simple: individuals who make
student loan payments have less money to spend on (or save
for) other things. The alleged link to the broader economy
is that decreasing spending by individual borrowers adds up
to less economic activity nationwide, a drag on the economy
that only worsens as more people borrow for college and debt
levels increase.

This worry exists independent of the fears of a student loan crisis discussed in the previous chapter. The borrower profiled in the vignette above feels constrained by the payments on his $45,000 in federal loans despite having a decent job. He does not struggle to make the payments on his loans, and still considers his education a wise investment, but thinks that the staples of adulthood, such as home ownership and marriage, are financially out of reach. These kinds of worries are at least as old as the federal loan system itself.[3]

There is no doubt that individual borrowers would be better off if they had less student debt, for example if college prices were lower or someone else paid for their education. That's just another way of saying that people prefer to have more money rather than less. But what are the broader economic effects of changes in how much college costs and how students pay for it? Do we have enough evidence to be confident that student loans are creating a drag on the economy? And might student debt also have important non-economic effects on borrowers, such as on their emotional well-being?

There is little high-quality evidence regarding the effects of student loans on borrowers and the economy, in large part due to methodological challenges. The effects of loans are hard to measure accurately and comprehensively because they work through many channels—enabling students to access an education, decreasing borrowers' ability to buy other things while increasing their capacity for earnings and spending in the future, and increasing the funds that institutions spend in their local economies, to name just a few. Beyond those effects, debt may impact economic decision making in less direct ways. Much of the concern about the impact of debt is implicitly focused on the emotional burden that it might impose on borrowers, thus affecting decision making.

The challenge in understanding the effect of debt on any number of outcomes is the simple fact that people with debt are different from people without debt in a number of ways— including in ways that we cannot observe. This means that any differences in their life experiences cannot necessarily be attributed to the differences in their use of student debt.

At the level of the individual borrower, there are a number of related causal relationships that would be valuable to know. For instance, how does defaulting on student loans impact a borrower? Or, how does student debt affect a borrower's credit score and ability to borrow (e.g., for a car or house)? However, we'll focus much of our discussion on exploring the broader question that has been posed most often in this discussion. Namely, how does the growing level of debt in the economy impact macroeconomic activity on different dimensions?

In this chapter, we discuss how loans could affect borrowers and the economy and explain the limitations of the existing evidence. A lack of high-quality evidence does not mean that none of the alleged effects of student loans are real, but it does require us to defer coming to strong conclusions until better evidence is available.

WHY EASING EDUCATION DEBT WON'T NECESSARILY HELP THE ECONOMY

Allegations that student loan debt is contributing to a plethora of social and economic problems are very difficult to substantiate with credible evidence. Claims about the effects of student loan debt largely rest on comparisons of individuals with and without student loan debt. The differences in observed outcomes—such as home ownership or mental health—are cited as evidence of an impact of student loan debt. For example, a 2014 Gallup poll of college graduates found that respondents who reported borrowing more for college reported lower levels of financial and physical well-being, on average.[4]

There are two main reasons why this approach doesn't tell us what we need to know about the effects of education debt. First, people who take on debt to pay for college are likely different from those who take on little or no education debt. Those who borrow likely do so for a variety of reasons, ranging from their parents' income and willingness to help them pay for college, to how much they worked while in college, to their willingness to take on debt. These factors are not all readily observed, making it difficult to take them into account in comparisons of the outcomes faced by borrowers and non-borrowers. Taking the oft-cited example of home ownership, we'd expect the individuals who have taken on education debt to buy homes at different rates than others even if they hadn't taken on education debt. That makes it difficult to draw inferences from straightforward observation of home buying behavior.

Second, the population of borrowers (and non-borrowers) has been changing over time. This means that studies tracking the outcomes of borrowers and non-borrowers over time are difficult to interpret. For example, if a decrease in home ownership is observed among borrowers, is that due to more people who prefer to rent joining the ranks of borrowers, higher levels of borrowing making it more difficult to secure a mortgage, or something else entirely?

It is useful to know how the circumstances of borrowers and non-borrowers have evolved over time, but this information does not tell us much about the impact of debt. In the previous chapter, we examined trends in average borrowing and income. This tells us something about how the financial situation of the average household with debt has changed over the last 20 years, but it does not tell us the impact that education debt has had on households. It could be the case that the average household with debt is better off financially in the long run, but would be even more better off had its members not taken on as much debt.

Widely cited evidence on the alleged impact of student debt on home ownership is a prominent example of the misuse of descriptive information on borrowers to reach conclusions about the causal impact of student loans. In 2013, the Federal Reserve Bank of New York (FRBNY) released an analysis of the relationship between student loan debt and home ownership.[5] The researchers reported that, by 2012, people with student loan debt had become less likely than those without debt to take on mortgage debt (a proxy for home ownership) by the time they reached age 30. This reversed the trend that had prevailed since the beginning of the data examined by FRBNY, in which individuals with student loan debt, who tended to be wealthier and more educated than their debtless peers, were more likely to own a home.

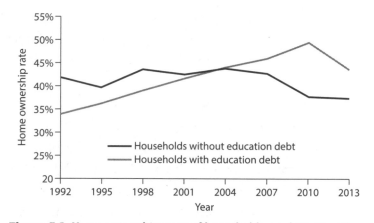

Figure 5.1. Home ownership rates of households aged 25–35 with and without education debt, 1992–2013
Source: Authors' calculations from Survey of Consumer Finances. *Notes:* Based on households where average age of adults is 25–35.

The FRBNY analysis provides useful descriptive information about the home ownership rates of individuals with and without student debt. But it is subject to both of the limitations discussed above, and is based on only ten years of data. A broader view, based on data that extend back an additional ten years, presents a different picture. Figure 5.1 shows that, prior to 2004, households aged 25–35 without education debt were more likely to own a home than households with debt. This reversed after 2004, and the FRBNY data on 30-year-olds (but not the data we analyze on 25- to 35-year-olds) indicate that it reversed again around 2012.

The FRBNY researchers called attention to the switch in higher home ownership rates from debtors to non-debtors, and the results received prominent media coverage in the *New York Times* and other outlets.[6] But the implicit argument that these data say anything about the impact of student debt on home ownership withers in light of evidence that the change highlighted by the FRBNY is a return to a pattern seen in the 1990s, a period when debt levels were lower than they are today. The bottom line is that these simple comparisons are informative but should not be used to gauge whether student debt is helping or harming borrowers.

Researchers working in this area are beginning to tackle the task of estimating the effect of student debt on rates of home purchasing in a way that takes into account the significant methodological challenges.[7] A recent study finds that the negative relationship between student debt and home purchasing disappears when the differences between the borrowing and non-borrowing populations are taken into account.[8] In essence, the authors do not find evidence to support the notion that student debt is causing a delay in home ownership and a depression of the housing market. Instead, they argue that the observed trends are consistent with two other explanations. First, home ownership rates were significantly impacted by the Great Recession, which was based largely on a disruption of the housing market. Second, the observed changes may be due to a structural change in the "social roles and expectations associated with young adulthood."[9] This new research begins to tackle this important question, but further work is necessary in order to draw strong conclusions about this relationship.

Our higher education system has quickly evolved into one that relies heavily on students taking out loans to finance their investments in education. Surely the growing phenomenon of holding education debt at the start of one's career will have very real effects, but the truth is that we don't know just yet what those effects are. In the meantime, it is still useful to consider *how* student debt might impact the economy through its effects on borrowers and other actors such as taxpayers and colleges. The vast majority of student debt is issued by the government, so it is most useful to consider the likely effects of different kinds of policy efforts aimed at reducing debt. The effects of such policy efforts will depend on how they go about reducing debt—the circumstances that would replace the status quo. We discuss three possible counterfactuals and show how they have different potential effects on borrowers and the economy.

First, the federal government could give money to borrowers by reducing the interest rates they pay, forgiving some of their debt, or providing grants that reduce their need to borrow in the first place. As the popular logic goes, borrowers would then have less to repay after graduation and would keep more of their paycheck to spend on purchases such as cars and houses. However, graduates with less debt may also choose lower-paying jobs, which would offset their increased spending ability.[10] But even if the total economic activity of borrowers increases, this logic still ignores the cost side of the equation. Government subsidies may increase consumption among those who receive them, but they necessarily decrease consumption among those who pay for them (through higher taxes).

The net effect of debt relief would depend on how the relief was structured, in particular who would reap the benefits and who would pay the price. A policy that reduces the debts of low-income college dropouts would likely have different effects than a policy that works mostly to the benefit of individuals with high debts and high incomes. The low-income borrowers struggling to make their payments would probably spend more of the debt relief, thereby providing a boost to the economy, whereas the high-income borrowers might be more inclined to save their government payout.

A second possible counterfactual is that student loan debt is reduced by discouraging spending on education. This could be accomplished by tightening loan limits in the federal lending program or increasing debt aversion by warning students about the dangers of borrowing. In this scenario, the benefits of having less debt have to be weighed against the foregone benefits of higher education. As we discussed in the previous chapter, investments in higher education pay large personal dividends, on average, which translate into additional spending by college graduates that stimulates the economy.

Once again, the net impact of reducing debt through reducing spending on college will depend on exactly how spending is reduced. Discouraging enrollment among students who would benefit from attending college could easily have a negative impact on the economy by reducing lifetime incomes. But encouraging students to attend colleges that provide better value (a higher return for a given price) could have a positive impact on the economy by maintaining the economic return to college while reducing the amount of debt needed to finance it (and any negative impacts of that debt).

The final counterfactual we discuss is reducing debt burdens by lowering spending by colleges and the prices charged to students. This could occur through some combination of market forces, such as providing information that increases competition on price, and government regulation, such as using the control that states have over their public institutions. The effect on borrowers' consumption is unambiguous: they would have more income left to spend (or save for future spending), assuming they were able to obtain the same quality of education at a lower price (and did not obtain a much lower-paying job).

But reducing debt by decreasing college spending would not necessarily be a boon for the economy. The reason is simple but often overlooked: money spent on higher education does not fall into a black hole. Tuition dollars are used to pay salaries, build infrastructure, and finance investments—all activities that potentially stimulate the economy just like consumption spending by graduates. It is not obvious whether the net economic effect of lowering college costs is positive or negative. It would depend on a number of factors, including the impact on educational investments (fewer students might go to college if quality falls); the impact of reduced prices on graduates' spending after college; and the impact of spending by colleges and universities on their local economies.

Watching the business news channels after the announcement of a positive change in national spending indicators illustrate that it's widely understood that spending is good for economic growth. Yet, we're broadly stuck on the notion that spending on education is bad. High price tags for college degrees certainly have undesirable outcomes, particularly with regard to access, but we should recognize that this concern is a separate issue. We can recognize simultaneously that tuition inflation is bad for encouraging college access for low-income students and also that higher spending on education isn't necessarily a drag on the economy.

Those concerned about the effect of student loans on the broader economy need to consider all of the economic effects of policy prescriptions, not just the benefits for students who will have lower debt burdens. The obvious benefits to students are often mitigated by the less apparent costs to the taxpayers who subsidize higher education (or the institutions that forego tuition dollars). None of the three possible counterfactuals to the status quo discussed above offer an unambiguous improvement of circumstances for the population as a whole. In other words, a world with less education debt is not *indisputably* better. Because the alleviation of education debt cannot be a costless exercise, policymakers need to be cognizant of the full ramifications of any intervention and recognize how the costs and benefits will be distributed.

IMPACT OF STUDENT DEBT ON BORROWERS

Student loans potentially impact the broader economy in part through the effect they have on borrowers. But loans can also have effects on borrowers that are not directly related to economic considerations. One recurring fear is that student loans are delaying marriage and childbearing.[11] Another is that education debt is having negative psychological impacts on borrowers.[12]

The effect of student loans on borrower well-being depends on the "relative to what" question about the counterfactual, just as the impact of policies aimed at lowering debt depends on how debt is reduced. Relative to grants, loans clearly leave individual borrowers worse off financially, all else equal. But loans can also have effects on career choices. A study of a wealthy, highly selective university that switched from loans to grants found that debt pushes students into higher-paying jobs and away from lower-paying "public interest" jobs.[13]

But what is the effect of loans relative to nothing? In theory, loans make college enrollment possible for students who cannot pay the tuition bills on their own. There is little high-quality evidence on this subject from the United States, but research on two other countries (Chile and South Africa) shows that making loans available can have a large, positive impact on college enrollment rates.[14] The evidence on the large economic returns to college, even for marginal students, suggests that students whose college enrollment is made possible by a loan likely also benefit in the long run, on average.[15]

But the long-run effects of education and debt should not be measured in financial terms alone. Education has many potential non-pecuniary benefits, but those benefits need to be weighed against the possible psychological and emotional impacts of debt.[16] For example, a 2015 study using nationally representative data found that individuals with more student loan debt reported lower levels of psychological health, controlling for other factors such as occupation, income, education, and family wealth.[17] This study takes an important first step in helping us to understand the emotional toll of student loan debt by attempting to control carefully for factors that are closely related to psychological well-being and debt. But it falls short of answering how debt, not wealth, impacts emotional well-being. This is because those nearly identical individuals differ not only in how much debt they are carrying, but also in how wealthy they are.[18] When one person has more debt than another person who is otherwise completely similar, the person with debt is less well-off. And we already know that wealth impacts emotional well-being. As a result, this research does not tell us whether student loan debt has psychological effects that are any greater than those imposed by other debts or financial obligations.

We think that the next step for research on the psychological and emotional effects of debt should be to measure the effect of debt while holding wealth constant. An example helps illustrate this seemingly semantic distinction. Consider two possible scenarios that an individual could face. In the first, she earns a monthly income of $1,000 and has no debt. In the second, she earns $1,500 each month but has to make a monthly $500 student loan payment.[19] The level of wealth is constant between the two scenarios, but the individual has a debt obligation in one and not in the other. By how much does the individual prefer the scenario in which she doesn't carry any debt?

This example is overly simplistic, but with a slightly more realistic example, the same framework could be used to measure how individuals' distaste for debt would change if the repayment period of the loan were different or if payments were building equity in an asset such as a car or a house. For example, holding wealth constant, do borrowers prefer smaller payments over a longer period of time or larger payments over a shorter period of time?

Evidence on these questions would be directly relevant to policy decisions about student loan programs, and will be informative as to how concerned we ought to be about the growing reliance on debt as a means for financing investments in higher education. Even if debt is an economically efficient mechanism for enabling access to higher education, it may impose emotional costs that counter some of its benefits.

Credible evidence that debt imposes a significant emotional cost to borrowers would suggest a role for policymakers to address this problem. One strategy to alleviate the emotional toll of debt is to change the tone of the public discourse on this issue. The often hysterical treatment of student debt by the popular media has almost certainly caused some borrowers to worry about their debts more than they would have otherwise. It may be possible to alleviate some concerns about debt through educational programs that help borrowers to better understand their circumstances and the safety nets that are available to them.

But changing the messaging around the existing student loan system may not be enough. Reforming the loan system itself may also reduce its emotional cost. For example, consider the disillusioned borrower with $40,000 in federal loans highlighted at the start of this chapter. This level of debt translates into a $411 monthly payment on a standard ten-year repayment plan, which may be burdensome for a new teacher in New York City (where living is expensive and the starting salary is $45,530).[20] But if the borrower were automatically placed into an income-driven repayment plan (as we propose in chapter 7), his payment would be $232, nearly half of the payment due under the standard plan.

Alternative ways to finance higher education, such as income share agreements or larger taxpayer subsidies for tuition (both of which we discuss in chapter 7), may be even more effective at alleviating any emotional burden of paying for college by reducing and even eliminating student debt as we know it.

Policy decisions driven by concern about the emotional effects of student debt would greatly benefit from a more robust research base on this issue. But this important dimension should remain front and center as policymakers consider ways to address the many real problems facing student lending that we document in the next chapter.

6

The Real Problems in Student Lending

The argument of the preceding two chapters—that there is no systemic student loan crisis—does not mean that all is well with student lending. There are serious problems with student borrowing—problems that are too often obscured by popular discussions around student debt.

These real problems can be seen in the stories of borrowers struggling to pay back their loans or suffering the consequences of default. Many of these borrowers are underwater on their student loans. Just as underwater homeowners owe more on their mortgage than their house is worth, underwater student loan borrowers owe more for their college education than the value of that education. These borrowers, many from disadvantaged backgrounds, would gladly return their degree or accumulated credits in exchange for their money back, if given the opportunity. Many should not have borrowed in the first place, but were provided no-questions-asked loans by the government to attend programs with abysmal records of student success.

Ending up underwater on student loans is a bad outcome for individuals regardless of whether they end up defaulting on their loans or avoiding default through alternative repayment plans that tie payments to income. But default on federal loans is a terrible outcome precisely because it is avoidable. Any amount of default, and the consequences it brings for borrowers' credit, is unacceptable when it comes to federal loans. The current default rate on student loans of 10 percent—representing 475,000 students in a single cohort who defaulted within only two years of entering repayment—is a national tragedy.[1]

Put simply, the current state of student lending in the United States diverges sharply from the ideal lending system described at the beginning of this book. A well-functioning market for student loans is one in which students think of higher education as an investment and make careful, well-informed decisions about whether and how much to borrow, and have access to a safety net that protects them from the risk inherent even in good investments. In the real world, students make uninformed decisions and are increasingly paying the price when their educational investments come up short. They face an uphill battle navigating the complexities of the federal loan bureaucracy, from when they first apply for debt through when they make their last payment.

BAD DECISION MAKING

Imagine a government that wants to encourage home ownership, so it gives anyone a mortgage of up to $138,500 to buy any house they want, regardless of the borrower's income or prior credit history. There are no appraisals or other restrictions on how much the home buyer can spend on a house. In fact, appraisals are not even possible because no historical information on house prices is publicly available. Buyers can only guess what houses are worth based on anecdotes and vague impressions. Finally, many buyers in this hypothetical place are financially illiterate. Even after signing their mortgage paperwork, most could not provide an accurate estimate of how much they borrowed.

Offering no-questions-asked loans in a market with severely limited information and non-savvy borrowers is clearly a recipe for disaster. But it's an unfortunately accurate description of the federal student lending system in the United States. Students can borrow up to a maximum of $138,500 for their undergraduate and graduate education, with no restrictions based on their likely ability to repay. Undergraduate students can borrow no more than $31,000 in federal loans in total, but their parents are often eligible to borrow much more, regardless of their income.[2] Stories abound of parents who suffer negative consequences after taking on federal loans to send their children to college.[3]

Students end up underwater on their student loans through a combination of bad decision making and bad luck. Students make predictably bad decisions when they borrow to attend colleges where they are unlikely to be successful enough for their loan payments to be affordable. A recent study found that much of the recent increase in student loan default rates stems from borrowers at for-profit and community colleges, where default rates have increased sharply over the last decade. Figure 6.1 shows that five-year default rates increased

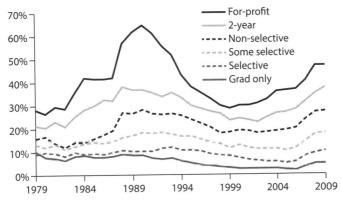

Figure 6.1. Five-year default rates, 1979–2009 repayment cohorts
Source: Data appendix to Adam Looney and Constantine Yannelis.

from 29 percent to 47 percent at for-profit colleges between 1999 and 2009; the corresponding increase at community colleges was 24 percent to 38 percent. Four-year colleges saw smaller increases, with the smallest increases observed among borrowers at selective colleges (8 to 10 percent) and students who only borrowed for graduate school (3 to 5 percent). The sectors of higher education with the worst outcomes today have always had relatively high default rates, with for-profit colleges topping the charts with a 65 percent default rate for the 1990 repayment cohort.

Students choose to attend an individual college, not an entire sector of higher education. And some individual institutions have truly abysmal borrower outcomes. As of 2014, borrowers from the University of Phoenix owed $35.5 billion to the federal government. But 45 percent of borrowers who entered repayment in 2009 had defaulted, and a grand total of only 1 percent of this group's debt was repaid. Contrast these numbers with those for the University of Southern California, a selective (and expensive) private university with a default rate of 5 percent (and where 20 percent of debt was repaid in the first five years of repayment).[4] These two institutions enroll very different student populations and have markedly divergent repayment outcomes, but the federal government lends on exactly the same terms to their students.

It is important to stress that bad decision making is not necessarily the fault of students—below we describe how it is nearly impossible to make good decisions without access to good information. And not all bad outcomes are predictable—some students simply get unlucky. An education that fails to pay off is bad for anyone, but borrowers are more likely to suffer given that they have to repay their debt without the returns that come from a successful educational investment. The upshot of increasing debt levels is that more students are facing that potential consequence of bad luck.

In an ideal world, borrowers think of higher education as an investment in themselves that will pay off not only through higher earnings but also improved health and happiness in the future. Some investments pay off better than others, and all entail taking on some risk. A well-informed borrowing decision thus requires undertaking a careful analysis of the costs and benefits of a particular program of study in higher education. But in practice good decision making is made nearly impossible by the lack of information available to potential college students.

Making an informed decision involving costs and benefits requires access to good information on what those costs and benefits are. Every college publishes what it charges for tuition, fees, room, and board, but students do not learn what they will actually pay until they apply to the college, are accepted, fill out a financial aid application, and then receive a financial aid offer. The situation has improved somewhat in recent years, as colleges have been required by the federal government to make net price calculators available, which allow students to fill out an online form and obtain an estimate of how much a college will charge them. But many of these calculators have been criticized as difficult to find and too complicated to use, and the average net price data that colleges are also required to publish have important limitations.[5]

Learning what a student will pay for college can be challenging, but obtaining a reasonably accurate prediction of post-graduation earnings is even more difficult. Success in the labor market is not the main reason that every student goes to college, but for many it needs to be a key consideration when they decide how much to pay for college and how much to borrow. A prospective poet likely expects to make less money than an engineer, but doesn't want to end up with more debt than he can reasonably expect to repay.

Ideally, students would be able to perfectly predict what their future holds if they pursue a particular program of study at a particular college. In reality, the best they can hope for is evidence of how similar students fared in previous years. Key pieces of information students should care about include their chances of graduating and their likely employment outcomes after graduation. Borrowing to attend a program where graduates earn an average of $50,000 at a college with an 80 percent graduation rate is likely a smarter bet than borrowing the same amount to pay for a program with average earnings of $25,000 and a 40 percent graduation rate.

The best way to assemble this kind of information is to link data on college students to data on their earnings after they leave college. Other ways to get the data, such as surveys, are sure to be less accurate and more expensive. The advantage of administrative data is that they are already collected by government and non-government entities for other purposes, and it is relatively easy to link the different data sources needed to examine the success of college graduates (and dropouts) in the labor market.

The actor in the strongest position to gather and publish this information is the federal government. The federal government makes the vast majority of student loans, so it knows how much students have borrowed and the colleges they are attending.[6] And it has detailed records on earnings gathered by the Social Security Administration (SSA) and the Internal Revenue Service (IRS).

Tracking the labor market successes and failures of college students should be as simple as linking the student loan data with the SSA or IRS earnings data, but for a federal law Congress passed in 2008 that explicitly prohibits the government from doing so. This law, which bans the creation of a federal "unit record system" of linked student data across multiple agencies, was passed with the strong support of the trade organization representing private, non-profit colleges. These institutions based their argument on privacy concerns, but they also may have been fearful of being held accountable for student outcomes by consumers and policymakers, perhaps in part because they charge higher prices than their public counterparts. Groups representing the other higher education sectors did not publicly support the ban but also did not aggressively oppose it.[7]

Legislation prevents the federal government from compiling a unit record system, but this law did not stop the Obama administration from introducing an important innovation in higher education data availability in the fall of 2015. For the first time, the U.S. Department of Education made institution-level earnings information available to the public. Students who shop for college using the "College Scorecard" web tool on the Department's website can now look up earnings information alongside other institutional characteristics, such as net price and graduation rate. Because of the ban on a unit record data system, however, these values were calculated by examining the earnings of students who participated in the federal aid program while they were enrolled. This means that the data do not reflect the outcomes of all former students. This is particularly true for institutions that serve a large number of students who do not apply for federal aid. Another important limitation of the federal data is that they only report average earnings for institutions and not for individual programs of study.[8]

Without a federal means of measuring the labor market outcomes of individual programs of study, a number of states have stepped up to fill the gap in information. States can link their education databases, which usually only include public colleges and universities, to their unemployment insurance systems, which track the earnings of workers in the state. These data systems miss students who leave the state after college—a problem that would be solved by a federal system—but enable states to produce valuable information.

Virginia has been a leader in assembling labor market information at the level of program of study. It is important to cut the data finer than an institutional average given the wide variation in earnings across different programs of study. For example, the average Virginia Tech graduate who works full-time in Virginia earns about $39,000 18 months after graduation. But this average is misleading to prospective students who plan to major in a field like English, where average earnings are about $28,000, or a field like computer engineering, where incomes average $55,000.[9] And recall that the earnings data currently made available by the federal government would only provide a single average for all federal aid recipients at Virginia Tech.

Virginia is particularly noteworthy because its data system includes both public and private universities. Table 6.1 shows the kind of information that a prospective business major might want to consult when considering where to go to college and how much to borrow. Graduates with business degrees who worked full-time in Virginia had average earnings ranging from less than $30,000 at three colleges to more than $40,000 at six institutions. Both ends of the earnings spectrum include a mix of public and private institutions.

It is important to emphasize that while the Virginia data illustrate the value of program-level earnings information, table 6.1 also highlights the limitation of using data from state systems that are not able to track graduates who leave the state. For example, at the University of Richmond, a private

Table 6.1. **Outcomes of Undergraduate Business Majors at Virginia Colleges, 2006–2010**

Institution	Sector	Graduation Rate (%)		Number of grads	Working full-time in VA (%)	Average wages
		4-year	6-year			
Averett University	Private	18	33	535	60	$52,534
Bridgewater College	Private	52	60	283	61	$31,331
Christopher Newport University	Public	50	65	823	63	$34,401
College of William and Mary	Public	83	90	1,001	33	$41,867
Eastern Mennonite University	Private	50	63	61	44	$32,615
Emory and Henry College	Private	33	48	66	45	$29,547
Ferrum College	Private	20	32	56	57	$27,850
George Mason University	Public	43	67	985	57	$44,508
Hampton University	Private	50	68	449	25	$33,692
James Madison University	Public	65	81	656	53	$36,767
Longwood University	Public	42	63	713	66	$34,484
Lynchburg College	Private	46	56	148	47	$33,503

(*continued*)

Table 6.1. (*continued*)

Institution	Sector	Graduation Rate (%)		Number of grads	Working full-time in VA (%)	Average wages
		4-year	6-year			
Mary Baldwin College	Private	39	39	163	62	$40,031
Marymount University	Private	44	57	313	42	$38,721
Old Dominion University	Public	23	51	816	56	$35,889
Radford University	Public	41	59	783	60	$34,279
Shenandoah University	Private	34	45	195	49	$41,380
University of Mary Washington	Public	66	74	683	47	$34,840
University of Richmond	Private	81	85	724	21	$46,872
Virginia State University	Public	25	46	302	49	$28,738
Virginia Tech	Public	61	83	915	46	$38,018
Virginia Wesleyan College	Private	37	44	270	62	$38,627

Source: SCHEV (labor market outcomes) and IPEDS (graduation rates).

Notes: Graduation rates are for class of first-time, full-time freshmen (all majors) who started at the institution in 2007–08. Labor market outcomes are averaged across all students who graduated between 2005–06 and 2009–10 with a bachelor's degree in "Business Administration and Management, General." Average wages are for the subset of graduates who were working full-time in Virginia.

institution with a graduation rate that exceeds 80 percent, only 21 percent of graduates with business degrees work full-time in the state, which is not surprising given that only 17 percent of these graduates were from Virginia.[10] As a result, data are not available for the majority of students, so it's impossible to say whether the average graduate from the University of Richmond does better than the average graduate from George Mason, which has similar average earnings but a majority of graduates staying in the state after college.

Virginia is not the only state that has assembled data on the economic success of college graduates. Arkansas, Colorado, Florida, Tennessee, and Texas have also made data available.[11] But in the other states, students who want to know how much they can expect to make if they successfully complete a given program of study are left to take a wild guess and hope for the best. That's no way to make one of the most consequential financial decisions of one's life.

It's clear that a lack of information has severely compromised students' ability to make smart college-going and borrowing decisions. Students haven't been able to make cost-benefit calculations with non-existent information on benefits and difficult-to-obtain information on costs. But as more information becomes available, will it be enough to solve the broader decision-making problem? The available evidence from education and other fields indicates that individuals too often do not understand, much less make use of, the information that is available to them. This means that simply providing more information to students is unlikely to change their behavior.[12]

A compelling piece of evidence of this problem comes from a nationally representative survey of first-year college students who took out federal loans to attend college. A surprisingly large fraction of these students were unaware of how much they borrowed when asked less than a year after they signed the promissory notes for their loans. Barely one-quarter of students could report their total borrowing within 10 percent of the correct amount. About half underestimated their debt by more than 10 percent, with the remaining quarter overestimating their debt. Figure 6.2 shows that this lack of knowledge of amounts borrowed persists across all sectors of higher education.

Perhaps the most dramatic finding from this survey is how many students who took out federal loans do not even understand that they have loans from the federal government. Fully

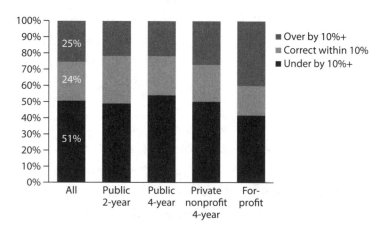

Figure 6.2. Accuracy of self-reports of federal student loans among first-year students with federal student loans
Source: Table 1 of Elizabeth J. Akers and Matthew M. Chingos, "Are College Students Borrowing Blindly?"

28 percent of first-year students with federal loans reported that they did not have any federal debt, and 14 percent of borrowers said that they did not have any debt at all. In a more limited dataset from a single institution, students were also often unaware of the price they (and their families) were paying for college.[13]

The fact that a majority of student borrowers do not know how much debt they have, and a non trivial number think they don't have any debt, makes it clear that simply providing more information is not going to solve the decision-making problem on its own. Students may lack not just the information needed to compare the costs and benefits of college, but also the knowledge, encouragement, and support to make sense of the information that is available to them. Student borrowers are being asked to make an important financial decision that requires the kinds of analytical abilities and critical thinking skills that may not develop until they attend college.

Students who do not understand how much they are paying for college and how much debt they are taking on are unlikely to be able to make savvy decisions regarding enrollment, major selection, persistence, and employment. Without knowledge of their financial circumstances, students are more likely to end up underwater on their student loans.

BAD LUCK

Bad decision making, whether it results from a lack of information or a lack of financial savvy, is not the only reason borrowers end up underwater on their student loans. Borrowers can also end up in a weak financial position due to bad luck. Bad luck can look like bad decision making in retrospect, but the key difference is that students who are unlucky experience unpredictably bad outcomes, whereas those who make bad decisions might have known better (at least with the right information and help making sense of it).

Bad luck can come in many forms. One type includes innovations in technology or policy that devalue certain skill sets. Imagine a student who obtains a certificate to work as an x-ray technician. But after he completes the program, a new x-ray machine is invented that does not require a certified operator. This person made a smart investment in his career but then a technological innovation hurt his job prospects. Changes in policy can have similar effects, such as the repeal of an import tax that leads to shifts in certain jobs overseas, leaving Americans who trained for those jobs without the income they expected to use to repay their education debts.

Broader economic conditions also impact workers' ability to repay their student loans. Recessions and the changes in employment rates and incomes that come with them cannot be predicted in advance. Borrowers are well-advised to leave themselves some wiggle room in their financial planning, but cannot reliably predict whether they will be a casualty of an economic downturn.

A different type of bad luck is an unanticipated change in a student's career goals. Imagine a student who enters college planning to study engineering. Perhaps she lives in a state with labor market outcome data available, so is able to choose a college with high average earnings among engineering graduates. The college she chooses costs a good deal more than other institutions, but this savvy student considers the costs and benefits and decides that the improved job prospects justify the higher price. But in her first year of college, this student discovers that her true calling is biology, so she changes majors. This student has done what college students are often advised to do: explore different fields and discover their passion. But she will have to pay back the debt she took on expecting an engineer's income with the significantly lower earnings of a biologist.

A more extreme example of the same problem is a student who obtains an expensive professional degree and then decides to change fields. A law school graduate with a large debt load who decides to switch to a lower-paying field is likely to struggle to pay the loans taken out for a degree he no longer needs or wants. This type of bad luck isn't the result of external forces but rather the unpredictable nature of changes in human preferences.

Bad luck is a fact of life, so why is it a problem in the market for student lending? In some respects, bad luck is the problem that the current lending system best protects students from in the form of income-driven repayment programs. These programs have shortcomings, which we discuss below, but they provide an opportunity for borrowers of federal loans to stay out of default by capping their loan payments based on their income. Borrowers of private loans do not have access to these programs, so bad luck can quickly push them into default as they do not have the option of selling back their degree, as they could with a house or a car.

Bad luck is still relevant to student borrowers because, even with income-driven repayment, they have to make payments for at least 20 years until any remaining balance is forgiven.[14] Consider the hypothetical engineer turned biologist above. Income-driven repayment will cap her monthly payments at 10 percent of her disposable income. But if she had not been unlucky, and had borrowed with a biologist's salary in mind, she may have not needed income-driven repayment, and only paid 7 percent of her income into her student loans.

More broadly, bad luck is increasingly relevant to the well-being of student borrowers because increasing debt levels mean that students are taking on more and more risk. The average household with a bachelor's degree has seen its average debt level increase from less than $7,000 in 1989 to nearly $22,000 in 2013 (figure 3.7). As students pay more for college and take on larger debt loads, they are more vulnerable to a stroke of bad luck from which it is difficult to recover. A $22,000 mistake is much costlier than a $7,000 mistake. The heightened cost of college has driven students to put more of their eggs into a single basket.

REPAYMENT PROBLEMS

The repayment system for federal student loans is in dire need of reform. This is made clear by the fact that so many borrowers fall through the safety net provided by income-driven repayment plans and default on their student loans. Economists

Susan Dynarski and Daniel Kreisman argue that the real crisis in student lending is on the repayment end:

> These four facts—moderate debt for the typical student borrower, the high payoff to college, high rates of default on typical loans, and higher rates of default among young borrowers—suggest we do not have a *debt* crisis but rather a *repayment* crisis. We have a repayment crisis because student loans are due when borrowers have the least capacity to pay.[15]

Why does this repayment crisis persist when the federal lending system offers a range of ways to reduce or delay payments in times of financial hardship? Because the repayment system is complicated, confusing, difficult to navigate, and managed by private servicers who are guaranteed customers regardless of the quality of the service they provide.

Borrowers who receive their first student loan statement from their loan servicer and find they cannot afford to make the payment have a number of options. The first is to do nothing, miss the payment, and hope they are able to make it up in the future. This strategy is likely to lead to default, but the borrower may not know that other options are available.

The second option is to request a deferment from the loan servicer. This option is routinely used by graduate students to defer payments on their undergraduate loans until they leave school. It is also available for borrowers who are unemployed or facing other kinds of financial hardship. During deferment, interest continues to accrue on some types of student loans but not others. Students who are not eligible for a deferment can request a forbearance, which stops payments for up to a year.[16]

A deferment or forbearance is a stop-gap measure to avoid default, but not a long-term solution. Income-driven repayment plans allow borrowers to permanently pay back their loans based on their income. But this option also comes in a variety of flavors. The Department of Education website listed five such plans, as of December 2015: (1) Income-Based Repayment Plan for borrowers who took out their first federal loans before July 1, 2014 (old IBR); (2) IBR Plan for borrowers who took out their first loan on or after July 1, 2014 (new IBR); (3) a plan called "Pay As You Earn" (PAYE); (4) Income-Contingent Repayment (ICR) plan; and (5) the Revised Pay As You Earn (REPAYE) plan.[17]

The most generous of these plans, new IBR and PAYE, cap payments at 10 percent of discretionary income, which is defined as the borrower's family income minus 150 percent of the federal poverty level for the borrower's family size.[18] This means that a single borrower with an annual income of $20,000 would make a monthly loan payment of about $20. A family of four with an income of $40,000 would pay about $30 per month.[19] Borrowers have to provide updated documentation of their income every year, and changes in income will change their payments. But after 20 years of payments, any remaining balance is forgiven.[20] The old IBR plan is somewhat less generous, capping payments at 15 percent of discretionary income and providing forgiveness after 25 years.[21]

The problem is that navigating among these IDR plans involves reading a lot of fine print to make a fairly complicated financial decision. A borrower who is facing the severe stress of financial hardship is unlikely to be in a strong position to sort out the finer details of discretionary income calculations, definitions of partial financial hardship, and required income documentation. Such a borrower may instead opt for a deferment or forbearance, which requires less bureaucratic wrangling but will not start the 20-year clock on forgiveness. Or they may be overwhelmed by the complexity of their choices and do nothing at all.

In theory, distressed borrowers do not have to sort out their options on their own. Loan servicers are supposed to help borrowers understand their options, and once a borrower has chosen an option it is the servicer's responsibility to make it happen. Borrowers don't enroll in an IDR plan or request a deferment by calling up the U.S. Department of Education; they do it through their servicer.

In recent years, student loan servicers have faced fierce criticism from advocacy groups and the Consumer Financial Protection Bureau. In addition to specific allegations of wrongdoing, such as overcharging members of the military, high default rates have been used as evidence that servicers are not doing enough to enroll struggling borrowers in income-driven repayment plans.[22] In late 2014, the U.S. Department of Education's Inspector General released a report critical of the department's lack of a coordinated effort to prevent defaults on student loans.[23]

Assessing the performance of the existing servicers is difficult because comprehensive data are not available. But a simple examination of the current system of student loan servicing reveals that a lack of competition among servicers creates weak incentives to serve borrowers well. Four companies service most federal student loans, and they are given a percentage of new borrowers based on measures of prior performance, such as the percentage of borrowers who are current on their loans and the results of a borrower survey.[24] However, performance scores are calculated based on the relative ranking of each of the four servicers. As a result, a servicer who performs very poorly on an important metric can still receive a sizable number of borrowers based on its performance on other metrics. And even a servicer that ranks dead last on every metric is given 10 percent of all new borrowers, although the government has the discretion to reduce that number to zero.[25]

The rules by which borrowers are allocated to servicers are not the only force inhibiting the quality of loan servicing. Innovation and competition are also limited by the fact that there are only four primary servicers. The existing players compete to some degree among themselves, but do not have to fear being disrupted by a loan servicing start-up that provides better service (and perhaps at a lower cost to taxpayers). And finally, borrowers are stuck with the servicer they are assigned, further weakening the incentives for the provision of high-quality customer service.

This is no way to run a bank, much less a massive lending program that affects the well-being of millions of Americans.

***

Borrowers of student loans who end up in financial distress get there through a combination of bad decision making, bad luck, and trouble navigating the repayment system. Media stories regularly feature struggling borrowers with six-figure debts, but the typical distressed borrower is actually on the other end of the borrowing spectrum. Borrowers with relatively small debts tend to have the most trouble repaying, in large part because they include many individuals who never earned their degree and the higher income that comes with it.[26] Defaulted loans also tend to have relatively small balances; a recent analysis found that 34 percent of borrowers who left school with $1,000 to $5,000 in debt in 2009 defaulted by 2014, as compared to 18–21 percent of those with more than $25,000 in debt.[27]

The broader point is that a borrower's financial position is at most weakly related to the amount of education debt she has. All else equal, less debt is better than more debt, just as more money is better than less money. But all else is rarely equal, and many borrowers with large balances also have high-paying jobs in fields such as law and medicine. Conversely, many borrowers with small debts have no degree to show for their investment and little income with which to make what may seem like small payments.

Conflating the amount of debt with the burden of debt is problematic because it can lead to policy solutions that give the most help to those who need it the least. Understanding where the real problems in student lending lie is a critical first step to solving those problems, the subject of the next chapter.

Solving the Real Problems

The first step to solving the real problems facing student lending is to stop trying to solve the broad-based student loan crisis that doesn't exist. Why has the rhetoric around student loans become so divorced from reality? The run-up in debt levels is surely part of the explanation, but an additional possibility is that popular narratives around student lending may have as much to do with who borrows as with how much they borrow.

In the early 1990s, student loan debt didn't vary much by household income. The average household in the bottom fifth of the income distribution had about as much education debt as the average household in the richest fifth: less than $2,000 in 2014 dollars.[1] But by 2013, that picture had changed dramatically, with the most affluent households exceeding $15,000 in average debt, compared to $10,000 for low-income households (figure 7.1). In 1992, middle-income households had the most debt, but in 2013 top-income households did. Essentially, student debt went from being a resource for the middle class to an instrument for the wealthy.

These changes in average debt levels increased the share of education debt held by the richest 20 percent of young households from 20 percent in 1992 to 29 percent in 2013. Looking

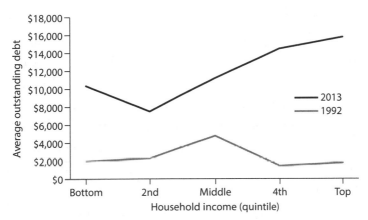

Figure 7.1. Average debt by income group, U.S. households, aged 20–40
Source: Authors' calculations from Survey of Consumer Finances. *Notes:* 2014 dollars. Income quintiles based on total income.

at all households, not just those aged 20–40, shows that the richest fifth held 44 percent of education debt in 2013.[2] Borrowers with high incomes are likely those for whom "student debt is the most formidable of first-world problems," as one commentator put it.[3]

An era in which students from low-income families used loans to supplement grants has given way to a system dominated by the wealthiest Americans, many of whom were born to affluent parents.[4] But this shift is not just a potential explanation for why student loans have received so much attention from journalists and policymakers in recent years. It is also the reason that efforts to offer broad-based "relief" to borrowers are likely to be regressive and wasteful.

The most prominent misguided efforts to help struggling student borrowers are to reduce the interest rates on existing loans under the guise of "refinancing." The idea, which has been vigorously promoted by Senator Elizabeth Warren, has attracted support from many prominent Democrats, including Hillary Clinton and Bernie Sanders.[5] It has intuitive appeal and makes for a good stump speech—the basic idea is that borrowers who took out loans when interest rates were higher should be able to obtain the lower rates that have prevailed in recent years, much as mortgages can be refinanced in the private market.[6]

But reducing interest rates on existing loans would provide a big handout to affluent borrowers and do close to nothing for truly struggling borrowers. Consider how different borrowers would be affected by an interest rate reduction from 6.8 percent, which prevailed on at least some federal loans from 2006 to 2011, to the 2015–16 undergraduate rate of 4.3 percent.[7] The average household in the bottom fifth of the income distribution, with about $10,000 in debt, would see a $13 reduction in their monthly payment, from $119 to $106.[8] But the average household in this group makes less than $13,000 in income, so will surely struggle to make any payment on its student loans. Households in an income-driven repayment plan do not make any payments at this income level, so the change in interest rate will have no impact. And households not in an income-driven plan are going to find themselves in trouble at any interest rate.

A family in the top fifth of the income distribution, with an average debt of more than $15,000, will see their monthly payment fall by $20. This government handout will add up to more than $2,000 over the life of the loan, but will probably not make much of a difference to the average family in this group in light of their average income of $173,000. The largest benefits will go to borrowers with large debt balances who are not in an income-driven repayment plan. For example, a lawyer with $100,000 in debt will see her monthly payments fall by $125, adding up to nearly $15,000 over the life of the loan.[9]

The argument has another fundamental flaw. Student loans *can* be refinanced, just like mortgages and auto loans. Many students are taking advantage of offers from the private market to do just that. Borrowers with good credit are able to refinance their federal loans with companies like SoFi and Earnest in order to pay lower interest rates. The reason that all borrowers don't find options to refinance their debt available is because the terms of their debt (the combination of interest rate and repayment benefits) with the federal government as the lender are far more generous than the private sector would ever be willing to provide.

The refinancing example makes clear that well-intended policies may please politically active constituencies but can have unintended consequences such as diverting limited public resources to those who need them the least. Addressing the real problems facing student lending is difficult because it requires both finding the right policy solutions and enacting them in the face of political pressure from groups that want help but do not necessarily need it.

The federal loan program has evolved from a small-scale effort aimed at boosting American competitiveness during the Cold War to a universal entitlement today (see chapter 3). Congress will have an opportunity to modernize the federal loan program when it reauthorizes the Higher Education Act, which was due for a rewrite in 2014. We believe there are a number of policy changes that would better support students as they make a financial decision that will affect the rest of their lives.

In this chapter, we'll present two sets of ideas aimed at mitigating the real problems facing the national system of student lending by making it fairer, better targeted, less risky, and more efficient. First, we'll discuss a policy agenda for simplifying the federal student aid system in ways that bring it back in line with the overarching goal of correcting the market failures that inhibit educational attainment while minimizing unintended consequences. This means adopting new policies that better address this goal as well as eliminating programs that are extraneous to this goal. The core of our proposal is consolidating existing federal aid programs into a single grant and single loan program that are better designed than any of the current programs.

Risk is the theme of our second, more ambitious set of reforms. As students pay and borrow more to attend college, they are taking on more risk. But our system of student lending does not adequately protect students from the growing risk they face of investing substantial sums in an education that does not pay off. We offer a set of reforms to the loan repayment system aimed at reducing the risk borrowers face, and discuss opportunities for experimentation with more innovative but largely untested ways of addressing this issue. These include shifting risk to taxpayers through increased public subsidies of college tuition and experimenting with new financing mechanisms that shift risk to the private sector.

We believe that both of these policy agendas offer ideas that merit consideration when Congress turns to the overdue reauthorization of the Higher Education Act, but we emphasize that we do not provide the level of detail and empirical analysis that will eventually be needed to translate ideas into actual policy. For example, we discuss the need for regulations that stop federal dollars from flowing to low-quality institutions, but avoid the thorny questions of how best to accomplish this difficult task. Our goal in this chapter is to lay out a set of high-level proposals that provide a starting point for discussions of higher education reform aimed at solving the real problems identified in this book.

ONE GRANT, ONE LOAN

The current system of higher education financing is the result of the accretion of federal, state, and institutional programs over many years. These programs are well-intentioned but produce a system that is confusing and difficult to navigate, and in many cases based on policies that do not meet the core purpose of a student lending system: correcting the market failures that keep promising students out of higher education. Congress could significantly improve on the existing system by streamlining all existing federal loans and grants into a pair of well designed programs.

A consolidated single loan program would end the current practice of students having to navigate the differing terms of unsubsidized, subsidized, PLUS, and other loan programs. The federal loan program should be returned to its historic mission of relaxing the credit constraints facing college students and their families, and should not be used to deliver subsidies. This means that the government should not pay interest on loans while students are in school, as it currently does on subsidized loans, and instead use those subsidies to increase the generosity of grants that directly reduce the prices students pay. It also means that the loan program should break even fiscally—and not profit from students or entail significant costs for taxpayers.[10] This is not because we seek to reduce subsidies to higher education, but because we believe that subsidies should be delivered through mechanisms that are efficient and effective at delivering subsidies where they are needed. Likewise, the student loan system isn't an appropriate tool for raising revenue for the government.

The single federal loan program should be a student loan program, not a parent loan program. The parent PLUS program, as we explain in chapter 2, makes loans available to families desperate to pay for their child's education but who ultimately will not be able to repay. One parent PLUS borrower explains the situation she was put in:

> You're at your wits' end, you want to help your kid, and this fairy princess appears on your computer and says: "Want some money?" [the parent borrower] recalled. You're like: Bingo! It's more than you can afford, but dammit, educa-

tion is important, right? Then four years later, you can't
believe how much you owe.[11]

The PLUS program should be eliminated, as creditworthy
parents can obtain consumer credit in the private sector. If
policymakers believe that the debt limits for undergraduate
students, which start at $5,500 for first-year students, are too
low, then they should increase those limits. Of course, requiring students to take on debt in their own name won't preclude
parents from helping their children to repay their debt. The
objective isn't to discourage this type of intergenerational
transfer, but rather to eliminate the pitfall of parents borrowing sums of money that they cannot reasonably afford to repay.
It also may make the cost of going to college more salient for
the student, which could encourage dependent students to
shop more carefully for college and, in turn, create stronger
incentives for colleges to keep prices low.

All federal subsidies of college students should be com-
bined into a single grant program that provides aid based on
students' financial circumstances.[12] Students cannot make good
decisions about where to go to college and how much to borrow without a solid understanding of how much they will
pay. They should at least be able to begin the college search
process with a firm understanding of how much help they
will get from Uncle Sam, without having to understand multiple federal grant programs, interest subsidies, tax-preferred
college savings accounts, tax credits, and the interaction of all
these benefits. The consolidated grant program should be mod-
eled after the Pell program, but could extend further up the

income ladder than the current program before benefits are phased out. Including more middle-class families in the program may be necessary to quell the political furor over eliminating education tax credits, tax-free 529 accounts, and other benefits that largely go to relatively affluent families.

Program consolidation will do little to help students who learn their eligibility too late, or fail to navigate the application process entirely. Students should learn their eligibility for federal grants and loans well in advance of applying to college and without having to complete any paperwork. There is broad consensus that the application for federal financial aid is too long and complicated, and that it should be shortened and simplified. We think it should be eliminated entirely. The federal government already has the information it needs to distribute grant dollars based on the income of students and their families. It could make these determinations based on average incomes over a long period of time (e.g., ten years) to capture the long-run ability of students and families to save for college and avoid the idiosyncrasies inherent in income data from a single year.[13]

In addition to reforming the process by which students apply for and receive grants and loans, the federal government should also make it harder for students to use federal aid to pay for consumption amenities. Currently, each college sets its own level of living expenses, which can vary significantly among colleges in the same geographic area. The federal government should standardize the calculation of living costs, so that grant and loan eligibility is linked to what it actually costs to live in an area rather than what each college says it costs.[14]

AN AGENDA THAT RECOGNIZES RISK

The discussion about higher education reform has long been dominated by the discussion of rising cost and rising debt, which we believe has missed an important issue: risk. Economic-minded analysts, ourselves included, frequently make the argument that it's wise to enroll in college when the increase in wages that will result from obtaining a degree outweighs the upfront costs. The problem with this simple rule of thumb is that it ignores the notion of risk.

Suppose for a minute that there was a stock available on the New York Stock Exchange with a historical rate of return of about 17 percent, far higher than the rate of return that most investors earn on their stock portfolios. Would we encourage young people to borrow in order to invest $30,000 in that stock? Of course not, because people widely recognize the importance of diversifying investments in order to avoid losing big if a single investment were to go bad. But in education we're encouraging students to do exactly that.

Risk cannot be eliminated, but it can be reduced and it can be shifted away from students. We discuss three strategies for reducing risk and how they could be implemented in the student lending system: information, regulation, and repayment reform. These reforms seek to mitigate the risk that students face when enrolling in college such that fewer individuals will have to face the bad outcomes that result from bad decision making and bad luck.

We then turn to two strategies for shifting risk. The first is increased public subsidies of higher education—including

making college tuition-free. This does not decrease risk overall, and may in fact increase it, but if students pay less for college then they face less of the cost of a bad outcome. The second strategy is to transfer risk to a third party through income
share agreements (ISAs), in which investors provide funding
for students' educations in return for a share of their future
income. We discuss the promise and pitfalls of ISAs, and suggest potential avenues for experimentation with this largely
untested innovation.

REDUCE RISK THROUGH INFORMATION, REGULATION, AND REPAYMENT

Prospective students and their families need access to better
information on the expected return on their educational investments. As we discussed in chapter 6, the federal government is in a unique position to provide this information by
linking data held by multiple agencies. Congress should abol-
ish the ban on the creation of a federal unit record data system, and instead compel the creation of such a system. Institutions that receive federal aid would be required to provide
limited student-level information to the federal government,
which would be linked to grant and loan data held by the Department of Education and to earnings data held by the Internal Revenue Service. Congress could simultaneously decrease
the regulatory burden on institutions by using the unit record
system to replace many of colleges' existing data reporting
requirements.

The unit record system would enable the federal government to provide information on labor market outcomes for each program of study in the country. Students would no longer have to rely on a vague sense that "college is worth it" (at worst) or the limited data currently made available by state and federal governments (at best) when deciding whether and how much to borrow. The provision of this information will also increase the likelihood that colleges compete on price and quality rather than prestige-based rankings and consumption amenities. This is particularly important in light of the concern that automatic income-driven repayment, which we discuss below, would make it easier for colleges to raise prices.

Providing more information will strengthen the market for higher education, but it will not change the fact that recipients of federal aid are spending other people's money when they go to college. This means that the federal government has a responsibility to ensure that taxpayer dollars are spent (and loaned) wisely. The Obama administration enacted "gainful employment" regulations aimed largely at for-profit colleges, an understandable move given the poor student outcomes at many for-profit institutions. But borrowers from other institutions, especially community colleges, have poor economic outcomes as well.[15] Congress should regulate colleges that receive federal aid based on their performance, regardless of their tax status.

Finally, there should be one repayment program, which is income-driven and automatic. Under this system, students would make loan payments as a percentage of their income.[16] Employers would withhold loan payments in the same manner as they withhold taxes, and remit the payments to the federal government. Since the payment amounts would be determined completely by the borrowers' earnings, the loan amount and interest rate would only affect how long borrowers make payments and not the monthly obligation. Borrowers would be unable to default on their loans, and there would be a much more limited role for servicers. Borrowers would still have the option of repaying their loans more quickly than the income-driven schedule if they so choose.[17] We would also introduce competition into the market for federal loan servicing by allowing borrowers to move their loan from one servicer to another if they are dissatisfied with their servicer. This would encourage the servicing industry to create innovations to address the myriad concerns that have been voiced by consumers.[18]

The main drawback of an automatic income-driven repayment program is that it could decrease students' sensitivity to the prices charged by colleges and thereby make it easier for colleges to raise their prices. A student who does not expect to make enough money to fully repay the loan would not care how much they borrow. These perverse incentives could be limited by extending the period of repayment prior to forgiveness for all borrowers (e.g., to 30 years), and by increasing the regulation of colleges' participation in the federal loan program, as discussed above.[19] Scaling back or eliminating forgiveness provisions also decreases the risk that the cost of these repayment programs will explode, leaving taxpayers to foot the bill.[20]

Several of the ideas we have discussed above already have bipartisan support in Congress. Republican Senator Marco

Rubio has joined with Democratic Senators Ron Wyden and Mark Warner to introduce "The Student Right to Know Before You Go Act," which would increase the availability of information on graduation rates, borrowing, and labor market outcomes accessible to prospective students.[21] Rubio and Warner have also introduced legislation that would enact a universal income driven repayment system.[22] Consolidation and simplification have also received bipartisan support, with a bill introduced by Republican Senator Lamar Alexander and his Democratic colleague Michael Bennet that is aimed at reducing the number of aid programs and simplifying the application process.[23]

Some proposals will surely be more controversial than others, but the existing consensus around many of these issues suggests that a core set of reforms aimed at simplifying the federal aid system and helping students make better informed decisions should be attainable even in our deeply polarized political environment.

SHIFTING RISK TO TAXPAYERS AND THE PRIVATE SECTOR

Because education is such an important tool for social mobility in this country, we believe that it's important to reduce risk in higher education. And we believe that the policies discussed above provide opportunities to do just that. An alternative to reducing the risk students face is to shift that risk to another party that can more easily withstand it, such as the government (i.e., taxpayers) or entities in the private sector.

But, as with any innovation, we must carefully consider the tradeoffs involved. We discuss the pros and cons of two strategies for shifting risk: increased public subsidies (or even free college) and income share agreements. The available evidence is too thin to support an endorsement of either strategy, but we believe that both offer fertile ground for experimentation.

A simple way to reduce the downside risk that students face is for the government to reduce the amount they pay for college by providing more generous grant aid to students or subsidies to public colleges. These plans can take many forms, but we focus on the idea of "free college" because it has received significant attention recently.[24] Plans for free college have proliferated from Democratic politicians and advocacy groups since early 2015, when President Obama released his plans to make community college free. The plans vary in their details, but generally involve significant federal money for states that increase their spending on public colleges and lower tuition.[25]

The basic idea is pretty simple: decrease tuition at public college by increasing direct public subsidies of those colleges. This decreases the risk borne by students because they have put less money on the table and thus have less to lose if their college experience is not successful. But it increases the risk borne by taxpayers who are making up the difference, and thus have wasted more resources if the public investment does not produce the expected number of additional college graduates.

An important advantage of the free college idea is its simplicity—it sweeps away confusion about sticker vs. net price by charging everyone the same, low price. Students no longer need to file paperwork to learn how much they will pay for tuition or worry about losing aid eligibility if their parents' income changes. Low-income students will likely still need to access the existing aid system to cover their living expenses, but the basic message of the program is clear: college is free in the same way that high school is free.

Extending full public support of education from high school into (at least part of) college would send a clear signal that society wants higher education to be accessible to everyone. But it also has a number of downsides. Free college would be free even for those who can afford to pay for it, and public colleges enroll many students from relatively affluent families.[26] Every dollar used to keep tuition low for families who can afford to pay is a dollar that could be used to reduce the living costs or provide other support for students for whom free tuition is not enough. This tradeoff may be warranted by the simplicity of free college and by the political support it attracts from higher-income voters, but it is a real cost of free college.

Free college plans could also distort the behavior of institutions and students in ways that potentially increase the overall level of risk in the higher education market. Institutions may find it easier to let costs continue to increase when the government is footing more of the bill. This concern would need to be addressed through policy design decisions aimed at ensuring that free college is more than just taxpayers throwing money at colleges with few strings attached. At the same time, recent history has shown that many states are willing to walk away from substantial federal subsidies. Nineteen states have still not accepted additional federal healthcare funding made available under the Affordable Care Act, largely due to political opposition.[27] Even if a Democratic administration managed to pass a federal-state partnership, it could end up excluding a substantial number of states that decline to participate.

The potential downside of free college for students is that it will lead them to make bad decisions about where to go to college by making the in-state public options so much cheaper than all other options. In states with a wide variety of public institutions, such as California, this may not be a problem. But a recent study found that a relatively small amount of financial aid (less than $2,000 per year), which could only be used at in-state public colleges, lowered the graduation rates of Massachusetts students by encouraging them to attend lower-quality colleges.[28] A free college policy limited to community colleges, like the one President Obama has proposed, could have a similar negative effect given the strong evidence base showing that students who start at a community college are less likely to complete a bachelor's degree than those who start at a four-year college.[29]

One way to reduce the odds of students choosing lower quality options than they otherwise would simply because they are free is to let students use their "free college" subsidies at a wider range of institutions than just the public colleges in their state. Students could be provided with a voucher that would make their in-state public college free, but would also provide the same (dollar) discount at other colleges, including private and out-of-state colleges. This version of a free college proposal would likely require regulation to ensure that colleges not controlled by the state do not increase their prices to capture the new grant money and that low-quality institutions cannot participate.

Free college might also force policymakers to reconsider the tradeoff between access and affordability once they are assuming all of the risk inherent in supporting students who are least likely to benefit from a college education. Under the current system, any high school graduate (or GED holder) can receive public subsidies to attend college. Under a free college policy, policymakers might decide to create stricter eligibility rules to focus resources on students most likely to be successful. The Obama proposal restricts eligibility to students who earn at least a 2.5 GPA, enroll at least half-time, and make steady progress toward a degree.[30] In other words, free college could shift some risk from students to taxpayers while shutting out the riskiest students entirely.

The cutoff between fully taxpayer-supported and partially taxpayer-supported public education is arbitrary, so it is reasonable for policymakers to question whether the amount of free and universal education should be extended, especially given the increasing necessity of a college degree for success in the labor market. Most if not all of the arguments against free college could also be made against free high school. But given the complicated tradeoffs involved, especially surrounding the need for targeting of limited public resources, we do not believe that free college is ready for prime time in the form of a large-scale federal policy. There are, however, clear opportunities for continued experimentation by states and a potential federal role in the form of support for pilot programs and rigorous evaluation.

Risk in higher education is largely shared by students and taxpayers. Taxpayers cover the cost of grants as well as student loans that are not repaid, but students face costs of college attendance (including foregone earnings) that are not usually fully covered by loans. We believe there is merit in proposals that would end the risk-free ride that colleges have had until this point. Colleges that consistently lend to students who fail to repay could be required to share in the cost of non-repayment or barred from accessing federal loan dollars in the future. But designing the right incentive scheme would likely be very difficult.[31] Consequently, we leave this as a subject for future research and turn to a discussion of how the private sector might bear more of the risk in the market for higher education.

The private sector currently provides very little of the financing, and thus bears little of the risk, in higher education. The experience of private student loans suggests that is a good thing, as private loans offer few of the consumer protections currently built into federal loans. But we think there are alternative financing mechanisms worth experimenting with that potentially harness some of the advantages of the private sector. Income share agreements (ISAs), in which students pay for college by selling "shares" in their future earnings, are one such innovation. ISAs are sometimes dismissed as a gimmick, akin to indentured servitude, but we think they merit serious consideration given their potential advantages over traditional loans.[32]

ISAs provide individuals with cash to pay for college in exchange for a promise that they will pay back a fraction of their earnings for a prescribed period of time to the entity that administered the agreement (e.g., 5 percent of earnings for ten years). Unlike a loan, where the total to be repaid is known up front, individuals who use ISAs to "borrow" money will pay back an amount that depends on their actual earnings. A graduate who earns less than expected will pay back less than the full amount of the initial funding, whereas graduates who earn more than expected will pay back more than their share. Income share agreements provide a tool for financing college and also serve as an insurance policy for the investment the student is making in her future self.

ISAs are not a new idea, with origins in a proposal by Milton Friedman in the 1950s, but they are not widely used in the United States.[34] From the student's perspective, ISAs offer protection similar to that offered by the existing income-driven repayment plans for federal loans, with the exception that high-earning students generally pay more under ISAs than under the traditional loan system. In other words, in the current system taxpayers bear the risk that borrowers will fail to repay, but do not share in the rewards when borrowers do well. Under ISAs, the entity that provided the upfront capital shares in both the risks and rewards.

The government could in theory administer ISAs, but we think they currently belong in the private market as an alternative to traditional private loans. Private loans provide no safety net for borrowers who cannot repay, such as income-driven repayment or even a fresh start through bankruptcy.

ISAs have neither of those downsides. Many critics of ISAs are concerned that students will agree to usurious terms because they do not understand this new product. That could certainly happen if adequate consumer protections are not put in place, but it's hard to imagine that this potential downside outweighs the known disadvantages of private student loans. Congress should balance the promise and pitfalls of ISAs by passing legislation that clarifies the legality of ISAs while also putting in place strong consumer protections.

Future research and policy experimentation will surely reveal additional upsides and downsides to the strategies for reducing and shifting risk that we discuss in this chapter, as well as innovations that are not yet part of the higher education policy discussion. These debates often occur in a politicized environment, where particular proposals have natural advocates and opponents. But we expect that the optimal policy design in a market as complicated as higher education will involve a combination of strategies that are often seen as being at odds, such as market-based accountability and government regulation, and public subsidies and private financing.

***

The greatest weakness of the government-based student lending system in the United States is that we ask far too much of it. The student loan system is used to subsidize low-income students by covering interest payments while they are in school, to provide windfall benefits to borrowers with high debts relative to their incomes through the forgiveness provisions in the income-driven repayment programs, to reward work in the public and non-profit sectors through the Public Service Loan Forgiveness Program, and to make consumer credit available to parents of college students.

Student lending should be returned to its core mission of providing students with access to their future earnings on terms appropriate for diverse constituencies, ranging from naïve 17-year-olds to low-income single parents. That means consumer protections on the front end, such as preventing students from borrowing to attend programs that will leave them unlikely to repay their debts, as well as strong safety nets on the repayment end, such as an automatic income-driven repayment system.

But even a well-functioning loan system is unlikely to accomplish all of society's goals for higher education. Consider a high school graduate from a low-income family who is not well prepared academically for college. She aspires to earn a bachelor's degree, but only 20 percent of students that begin college with her level of preparation make it to graduation. The existing loan program would allow this student (and possibly her parents) to take on debts that they are unlikely to be able to repay, especially given the student's 80 percent chance of dropping out.

A redesigned student loan program aimed at encouraging students to make good investments and avoid bad ones would not encourage this student to take on much debt. It may even shut her out entirely. If, as a society, we want to give this student a chance at earning a college degree, we shouldn't do that by saddling her with debt we know she's unlikely to repay and then suggesting she enter income-based repayment for 20 years. Instead, we should provide an upfront grant to cover the part of the cost that doesn't have an expected financial return but pays for our national commitment to ensuring access to opportunity. This could be done by making public colleges free, or through a carefully targeted grant program.

Borrowers are not the only group in need of protection from the dangers of student borrowing. U.S. taxpayers, who are owed more than $1 trillion in outstanding federal education debt, should not suffer enormous losses on these loans. The expansion of income-driven repayment programs is likely to entail significant costs to taxpayers as more borrowers participate.[34] That is why it is critical that these programs be designed to provide a safety net to those who need it the most and not provide windfall benefits to those who merely wish they had less debt. The willingness of the government to respond to political pressure and provide costly benefits to previous borrowers is also a reason why greater participation by the private sector is desirable, provided that it is accompanied by strong consumer protections.

Student loans open the university gates to millions of Americans every year. When used well, they enable students to close the gap between their financial resources and college prices by tapping into their future earnings. But for too many students, they become a lifelong reminder of their failed foray into higher education. The challenge policymakers must address is to create a modernized system of student lending in which debt remains a critical tool that does less harm and more good.

Notes

CHAPTER 1: A BRIEF INTRODUCTION TO STUDENT LOANS

1. Janet S. Hansen, *Student Loans: Are They Overburdening a Generation?* (New York: College Board, 1987), iv.

2. See chapter 3 for data sources.

3. Annie Lowrey, "Student Debt Slows Growth as Young Spend Less," *New York Times*, May 10, 2013, accessed July 6, 2015, http://www.nytimes.com/2013/05/11/business/economy/student-loan-debt-weighing-down-younger-us-workers.html; Elizabeth Dwoskin, "Will You Marry Me (After I Pay Off My Student Loans)?" *Bloomberg Business*, March 28, 2012, accessed July 6, 2015, http://www.bloomberg.com/bw/articles/2012-03-28/will-you-marry-me-after-i-pay-off-my-student-loans; Meera Louis, "Student Debt Puts Young Entrepreneurs on Hold," *Bloomberg Business*, June 20, 2013, accessed July 6, 2015, http://www.bloomberg.com/bw/articles/2013-06-20/student-debt-puts-young-entrepreneurs-on-hold.

4. Figure 1.1 is in 2014 dollars, but total student debt passed the $1 trillion mark in both current and 2014 dollars in 2013 (Q3 in 2013 dollars and Q1 in 2014 dollars).

5. Rohit Chopra, "Too Big to Fail: Student Debt Hit a Trillion," Consumer Financial Protection Bureau, March 21, 2012, accessed July 6, 2015, http://www.consumerfinance.gov/blog/too-big-to-fail-student-debt-hits-a-trillion/.

6. "63,000 Delinquent on Student Loans," Associated Press, April 10, 1982, accessed July 6, 2015, http://www.nytimes.com/1982/04/10/us/63000-delinquent-on-student-loans.html; Steven R. Weisman, "Reagan Attacks Critics Over Cut in Student Aid," *New York Times*, April 11, 1982, accessed July 6, 2015, http://www.nytimes.com/1982/04/11/us/reagan-attacks-critics-over-cut-in-student-aid.html.

7. Hansen, *Student Loans*, pp. iv–v.

8. One possible justification is what economists call consumption smoothing. If a college student expects to make a lot of money in the future, they might think it wise to borrow more than absolutely necessary now so that they can enjoy a better standard of living rather than living "like a student" now and then having more money than they need in the future. Of course, students are already betting on a higher future income and increasing the size of the bet increases the risk they are taking on.

9. Many parents who invest in their children's education may believe that their children will provide them financial support later in life. In this way, borrowing to finance another person's education could also be seen as an investment.

10. Milton Friedman, "The Role of Government in Education (1955)," Friedman Foundation for Educational Choice, accessed July 6, 2015, http://www.edchoice.org/The-Friedmans/The-Friedmans-on-School-Choice/The-Role-of-Government-in-Education-(1995).aspx.

CHAPTER 2: WHAT DOES STUDENT BORROWING IN THE UNITED STATES REALLY LOOK LIKE?

1. See, for example, Andrew Martin and Andrew W. Lehren, "A Generation Hobbled by the Soaring Cost of College," *New York Times*, May 12, 2012, accessed June 26, 2015, http://www.nytimes.com/2012/05/13/business/student-loans-weighing-down-a-generation-with-heavy-debt.html; Adam Davidson, "It's Official: The Boomerang Kids Won't Leave," *New York Times*, June 20, 2014, accessed June 26, 2015, http://www.nytimes.com/slideshow/2014/06/22/magazine/22boomerang_ss-nytnowcopy.html.

2. Matt McDonald and Pat Brady, "The Plural of Anecdote Is Data (Except for Student Debt)," Hamilton Place Strategies, accessed June 26, 2015, http://hamiltonplacestrategies.com/sites/default/files/newsfiles/Media%20coverage%20of%20student%20debt_1.pdf.

3. Authors' calculations from NPSAS 2011–12, using total debt in 2014 dollars. The corresponding percentages for borrowers only are 98% and 70%.

4. "Total Federal and Nonfederal Loans over Time," College Board, accessed June 26, 2015, http://trends.collegeboard.org/student-aid/figures-tables/total-federa-nonfederal-loans-time. The federal government also made $10.3 billion in loans to parents of undergraduate students (PLUS) in 2013–14. We briefly discuss parent loans later in this chapter.

5. "Federal Student Loan Portfolio," U.S. Department of Education, accessed December 14, 2015, https://studentaid.ed.gov/about/data-center

/student/portfolio. This total includes lending to parents, so slightly over-states the balance of loans held by students for their own education.

6. "Student Loan Debt Clock," FinAid, accessed December 14, 2015, http://www.finaid.org/loans/studentloandebtclock.phtml.

7. In the 2011–12 NPSAS, 51% of domestic undergraduates are classified as independent. 74% of dependent students were enrolled mostly full-time, as compared to 49% of independent students.

8. Stacey Patton, "A Graduate Student with $88,000 in Student Loans Speaks Out About College Debt," *Chronicle of Higher Education*, March 19, 2012, accessed June 26, 2015, http://chronicle.com/article/A-Graduate-Student-With/131251/.

9. Students from countries other than the United States are generally not eligible for federal loans. There are some additional restrictions, which are detailed in "Who Gets Aid," U.S. Department of Education, accessed June 26, 2015, https://studentaid.ed.gov/eligibility.

10. Financial need is calculated by a federal formula that takes into account both income and the price charged by the college. As a result, students can be eligible for greater subsidized loans (where the government pays the interest while they are enrolled) by being from a lower income family or by attending a more expensive college.

11. This analysis ignores federal Perkins loans, which are made by individual schools based on student need and made up only 1% of total borrowing in 2013–14.

12. This rate changes each academic year and is set based on a market interest rate.

13. We note that outstanding debt can exceed initial borrowing, potentially by large amounts, if interest accumulates faster than students make payments (e.g., through deferral, forbearance, or income-driven repayment). However, we also note that the outstanding balance on the loan is less important for students in income-driven repayment programs given the forgiveness provisions of these programs.

14. PLUS borrowing is limited to the cost of attendance as defined by the college (including living expenses) minus any other aid received. PLUS loans also charge a 4.29% origination fee, as compared to the 1.07% fee on other federal student loans.

15. These calculations ignore the interest that accumulates on some federal loans while students are still in school. A dependent undergraduate who borrows the maximum each year for four years would have a monthly payment per $10,000 borrowed of approximately $106–$114, depending on her level of eligibility for in-school interest subsidies.

16. "Standard Plan," U.S. Department of Education, accessed June 26, 2015, https://studentaid.ed.gov/repay-loans/understand/plans/standard.

17. "Repayment Plans," U.S. Department of Education, accessed June 26, 2015, https://studentaid.ed.gov/repay-loans/understand/plans.

18. "Deferment and Forbearance," U.S. Department of Education, accessed June 26, 2015, https://studentaid.ed.gov/repay-loans/deferment-forbearance.

19. Parents who can borrow against the equity in their house may be able to do so at a lower interest rate (taking into account the tax deductibility of mortgage interest) than federal student loans. It is difficult to study this behavior because it is not measured in federal education data collections such as the NPSAS. A 2008 survey of the parents of traditional-age undergraduates found that only 3% reported drawing on their home equity to help pay for college (Doug Lederman, "How Americans Pay for College," *Inside Higher Ed*, August 20, 2008, accessed December 7, 2015, https://www.insidehighered.com/news/2008/08/20/pay).

20. Rachel Fishman, "The Parent Trap: Parent PLUS Loans and Intergenerational Borrowing," New America, January 2014, accessed June 26, 2015, https://static.newamerica.org/attachments/748-the-parent-trap/Corrected-20140110-ParentTrap.pdf.

21. "Direct PLUS Loans and Adverse Credit," U.S. Department of Education, accessed June 26, 2015, https://studentaid.ed.gov/sites/default/files/plus-adverse-credit.pdf.

22. Eight percent of the parents of Pell grant recipients borrowed PLUS loans in 2012 (Fishman, "The Parent Trap").

23. Fishman, "The Parent Trap."

24. "Private Student Loans," Consumer Financial Protection Bureau, August 29, 2012, accessed June 26, 2015, http://files.consumerfinance.gov/f/201207_cfpb_Reports_Private-Student-Loans.pdf; "The MeasureOne Student Loan Performance Report Q3 2014," MeasureOne, accessed June 26, 2015, http://www.measureone.com/system/tdf/reports/MeasureOne%20Private%20Student%20Loan%20Performance%20Report%20Q3%202014%20121614%20FINAL.pdf?file=1.

25. Rohit Chopra, "Annual Report of the CFPB Student Loan Ombudsman," Consumer Financial Protection Bureau, October 16, 2014, accessed June 26, 2015, http://files.consumerfinance.gov/f/201410_cfpb_report_annual-report-of-the-student-loan-ombudsman.pdf.

26. "Percentage of Undergraduate and Graduate Students Borrowing Private Loans over Time," College Board, accessed June 26, 2015, http://trends.collegeboard.org/student-aid/figures-tables/percentage-undergraduate-and-graduate-students-borrowing-private-loans-over-time. These data

are based on NPSAS data and may suffer from self-reporting errors, as we discuss below (Elizabeth J. Akers and Matthew M. Chingos, "Are College Students Borrowing Blindly?" Brookings Institution, December 2014, accessed June 26, 2015, http://www.brookings.edu/~/media/research/files/reports/2014/12/10-borrowing-blindly/are-college-students-borrowing-blindly_dec-2014.pdf).

27. Susan Dynarski, "We're Frighteningly in the Dark About Student Debt," *New York Times*, March 20, 2015, accessed June 26, 2015, http://www.nytimes.com/2015/03/22/upshot/were-frighteningly-in-the-dark-about-student-debt.html.

28. "Federal Student Loan Portfolio."

29. Adam Looney and Constantine Yannelis, "A Crisis in Student Loans? How Changes in the Characteristics of Borrowers and the Institutions They Attended Contributed to Loan Defaults," *Brookings Papers on Economic Activity* Conference Draft, September 2015, accessed December 14, 2015, http://www.brookings.edu/~/media/projects/bpea/fall-2015_embargoed/conferencedraft_looneyyannelis_studentloandefaults.pdf.

30. For a more detailed discussion of these datasets, see Beth Akers and Matthew M. Chingos, "Is a Student Loan Crisis on the Horizon?" Brookings Institution, June 2014, accessed June 26, 2015, http://www.brookings.edu/research/reports/2014/06/24-student-loan-crisis-akers-chingos.

31. Aggregate data suggest that borrowing today is likely lower than in 2011–12, with total borrowing falling 11% between 2011–12 and 2013–14 ("Total Federal and Nonfederal Loans over Time," College Board, accessed June 26, 2015, http://trends.collegeboard.org/student-aid/figures-tables/total-federa-nonfederal-loans-time).

32. Akers and Chingos, "Are College Students Borrowing Blindly?"

33. NPSAS calculates each student's total borrowing as the maximum of her self-report of her total borrowing and the government's record of her total federal borrowing. This will correct for students who under-report their total debt, but will introduce errors for students who over-report their total debt. Unfortunately there is not a straightforward fix to this problem because NPSAS only contains administrative records on federal borrowing, not total borrowing.

34. See the third photo in the slideshow in Davidson, "It's Official: The Boomerang Kids Won't Leave."

35. Alexandria Walton Radford, Lutz Berkner, Sara C. Wheeless, and Bryan Shepherd, "Persistence and Attainment of 2003–04 Beginning Postsecondary Students: After 6 Years," National Center for Education Statistics, December 2010, http://nces.ed.gov/pubs2011/2011151.pdf.

36. We combine two-year and four-year for-profit institutions for ease of presentation and because their average borrowing levels are similar.

37. Authors' calculations from the 2013 Survey of Consumer Finances.

CHAPTER 3: HOW DID WE GET HERE?

1. Current Population Survey, 1993–2013.

2. Authors' analysis of NPSAS 1990 and 2012. Average borrowing (per year) among all undergraduate students (including non-borrowers) increased from $1,172 to $3,151 (in 2014 dollars) over this period.

3. Authors' analysis of households with average age 20–40 in the 1992 and 2013 Survey of Consumer Finances; amounts are per adult in the household and are in 2014 dollars.

4. Part of increased borrowing behavior could reflect changes in the composition of college students. For example, we would expect borrowing to increase if the marginal students induced to attend college in more recent years are more financially needy. This is intuitively plausible, but work by Martha Bailey and Susan Dynarski indicates that while low-income students are more likely to attend college than they were in previous years, college attendance rates have increased by even greater amounts among students from high-income families, leaving the relative income composition of the college-going population largely unchanged (Martha J. Bailey and Susan M. Dynarski, "Gains and Gaps: Changing Inequality in U.S. College Entry and Completion," National Bureau of Economic Research Working Paper No. 17633, December 2011). Brad Hershbein and Kevin Hollenbeck report that dependent undergraduate students saw an increase in average financial resources between 1990 and 2008, whereas independent students saw a decrease (Brad Hershbein and Kevin M. Hollenbeck, "The Distribution of College Graduate Debt, 1990–2008: A Decomposition Approach," in *Student Loans and the Dynamics of Debt*, ed. Brad Hershbein and Kevin M. Hollenbeck (Kalamazoo: W.E. Upjohn Institute for Employment Research, 2015, 53–116).

5. Authors' analysis of SCF data; for details of methodology, see Beth Akers and Matthew M. Chingos, "Is a Student Loan Crisis on the Horizon?" Brookings Institution, June 2014, accessed June 26, 2015, http://www.brookings.edu/research/reports/2014/06/24-student-loan-crisis-akers-chingos.

6. Robert A. Caro, *The Years of Lyndon Johnson: The Path to Power* (New York: Knopf, 1982), 163–164.

7. Janet S. Hansen, "The Politics of Federal Scholarships: A Case Study of the Development of General Grant Assistance for Undergraduates" (PhD diss., Princeton University, 1977), 149.

8. "Education Timeline for 1963–1968," Lyndon Baines Johnson Presidential Library, accessed June 26, 2015, http://www.lbjlib.utexas.edu/johnson /lbjforkids/edu_timeline.shtm.

9. John U. Monro, "Untapped Resource: Loans for Student Aid," *College Board Review* Winter (1956), 14.

10. "Seven Years' Experience with Student Loans" New York: Harmon Foundation, 1929.

11. "How Did We Get Here: Growth of Federal Student Loans (Part 1)," Lumina Foundation, accessed June 26, 2015, https.//www.youtube.com /watch?v=6Cha6bWhuD0.

12. Rupert Wilkinson, *Aiding Students, Buying Students: Financial Aid In America* (Nashville, TN: Vanderbilt University Press, 2005), 53–54.

13. The Perkins program expired in late 2015. As a result, disbursements will wind down in the coming years unless Congress decides to extend it.

14. "How Did We Get Here: Growth of Federal Student Loans (Part 1)," 4.

15. Lawrence E. Gladieux, "Federal Student Aid Policy: A History and an Assessment," *Financing Postsecondary Education: The Federal Role— October 1995*, U.S. Department of Education, accessed December 14, 2015, https://www2.ed.gov/offices/OPE/PPI/FinPostSecEd/gladieux.html.

16. Janet S. Hansen, *Student Loans: Are They Overburdening A Generation?* (New York: College Board, 1987), 4; "How Did We Get Here: Growth of Federal Student Loans (Part 1)."

17. "History of Student Financial Aid," FinAid, accessed June 26, 2015, http://www.finaid.org/educators/history.phtml.

18. For evidence that unsubsidized loans were a larger driver of growth in student loans among bachelor's degree recipients in the late 1990s than in the mid-1990s, see Hershbein and Hollenbeck, "The Distribution of College Graduate Debt, 1990–2008," 53–116.

19. The rapid reduction in federal grants beginning in the mid-1970s was due primarily to a decrease in veterans' benefits. Excluding grants to veterans and the military, federal loans exceeded federal grants from the beginning of the data series (1970) to 1973 and from 1980 to the present (authors' calculations based on data provided by Sandy Baum).

20. Sandy Baum, Diane Cardenas Elliott, and Jennifer Ma, *Trends in Student Aid 2014* (New York: College Board, 2014), accessed June 26, 2015, https://secure-media.collegeboard.org/digitalServices/misc/trends/2014 -trends-student-aid-report-final.pdf; George B. Bulman and Caroline M. Hoxby, "The Returns to the Federal Tax Credits for Higher Education," National Bureau of Economic Research Working Paper No. 20833, January 2015.

21. Hansen, "The Politics of Federal Scholarships," 149

22. "How Did We Get Here: Growth of Federal Student Loans (Part 1)."

23. These concerns date back at least to the 1950s, when a group of Boston executives, worried about their ability to send their children to college, created a loan guarantee program (Wilkinson, *Aiding Students, Buying Students*, 53–54).

24. Authors' calculations from NPSAS 1990 and 2012.

25. These data only include tuition and fees. We set aside room and board charges because they are reported by the colleges and do not necessarily reflect the actual living costs of students who live off-campus (who represent the vast majority of all college students; our calculations from the 2012 NPSAS indicate that, among undergraduate students attending a single institution, 13% lived on campus, 50% lived off campus, and 37% lived with parents). The measurement challenge is made clear by the fact that reported room and board charges have increased by 80–88% since 1963 (after adjusting for inflation). For additional discussion of this set of issues, see Robert Kelchen, Sara Goldrick-Rab, and Braden Hosch, "The Costs of College Attendance: Trends, Variation, and Accuracy in Institutional Living Cost Allowances" (paper presented at the annual meeting of the Association of Public Policy and Management, Albuquerque, New Mexico, November 6–8, 2014).

26. Sandy Baum and others, "Beyond Need and Merit: Strengthening State Grant Programs," Brown Center on Education Policy, Brookings Institution, May 2012, accessed October 6, 2015, http://www.brookings.edu/~ /media/research/files/reports/2012/5/08%20grants%20chingos%20white hurst/0508_state_grant_chingos_whitehurst.pdf.

27. Authors' calculations from NPSAS. High- and low-income refer to top and bottom quartiles of the college-going population, respectively.

28. Hershbein and Hollenbeck, "The Distribution of College Graduate Debt, 1990–2008," 53–116; email correspondence with Brad Hershbein regarding unpublished updated paper that includes 2012 data.

29. Tables 330.10 and 330.50 of 2013 Digest of Education Statistics, U.S. Department of Education, inflated to 2014 dollars. The changes are about the same in percentage terms (85% for graduate tuition and 87% for undergraduate tuition).

30. The total cost of attendance (in 2014 dollars, including room and board) increased by $10,735 for graduate students between 1995–96 and 2011–12 (Jennie H. Woo and Stacy Shaw, "Trends in Graduate Student Financing: Selected Years, 1995–96 to 2011–12," U.S. Department of Education, January 2015, accessed June 26, 2015, http://nces.ed.gov/pubs2015 /2015026.pdf). Over this same period, average net price increased by $8,524. The corresponding increases for undergraduates are $8,249 for list price and $4,640 for net price (Laura Horn and Jonathan Paslov, "Trends in

Student Financing of Undergraduate Education: Selected Years, 1995–96 to 2011–12," U.S. Department of Education, September 2014, accessed June 26, 2015, http://nces.ed.gov/pubs2014/2014013rev.pdf).

31. Sandy Baum and Jennifer Ma, *Trends in College Pricing 2014* (New York: College Board, 2014), accessed June 26, 2015, https://secure-media .collegeboard.org/digitalServices/misc/trends/2014-trends-college-pricing -report-final.pdf, figure 8.

32. Monro, "Untapped Resource," 15.

33. Lesley J. Turner, "The Road to Pell is Paved with Good Intentions: The Economic Incidence of Federal Student Grant Aid," unpublished manuscript, 2014; Bridget Terry Long, "How Do Financial Aid Policies Affect Colleges? The Institutional Impact of the Georgia HOPE Scholarship," *Journal of Human Resources* 39 (2004): 1045–1066.

34. Stephanie Riegg Cellini and Claudia Goldin, "Does Federal Student Aid Raise Tuition? New Evidence on For-Profit Colleges," *American Economic Journal: Economic Policy* 6 (2014): 174.

35. Bulman and Hoxby, "The Returns to the Federal Tax Credits." For contrary evidence, see Nicholas Turner, "Who Benefits from Student Aid? The Economic Incidence of Tax-Based Federal Student Aid," *Economics of Education Review* 31 (2012): 463–481.

36. David O. Lucca, Taylor Nadauld, and Karen Shen, "Credit Supply and the Rise in College Tuition: Evidence from the Expansion in Federal Student Aid Programs," Federal Reserve Bank of New York Staff Report No. 733, July 2015, accessed July 9, 2015, http://www.newyorkfed.org/research/staff_reports /sr733.pdf. This paper examines published prices rather than net prices, and appears to rely on a mistaken assumption about loan policy (that unsubsidized loans were not available to undergraduates before 2007, which is not true).

37. William Baumol and William Bowen, *Performing Arts, The Economic Dilemma: A Study of Problems Common to Theater, Opera, Music, and Dance* (New York: Twentieth Century Fund, 1966).

38. Benjamin Ginsburg, *The Fall of the Faculty: The Rise of the All-Administrative University and Why It Matters* (Oxford: Oxford University Press, 2011).

39. Brian Jacob, Brian McCall, Kevin M. Stange, "College as Country Club: Do Colleges Cater to Students' Preferences for Consumption?" National Bureau of Economic Research Working Paper No. 18745, 2013.

40. Baum and Ma, figure 16B (inflated to 2014 dollars).

41. Thomas J. Kane, Peter R. Orszag, and David L. Gunter, "State Fiscal Constraints and Higher Education Spending: The Role of Medicaid and the Business Cycle," Urban-Brookings Tax Policy Center Discussion Paper No. 11, May 2003.

42. Baum and Ma, *Trends in College Pricing 2014*, figure 17B.

43. Hershbein and Hollenbeck, "The Distribution of College Graduate Debt, 1990–2008," 53–116

44. Baum and Ma, *Trends in College Pricing 2014*, Figure 19A (inflated to 2014 dollars).

45. Spending per student actually *fell* by 7% at community colleges.

46. Ronald G. Ehrenberg, "American Higher Education in Transition," *Journal of Economic Perspectives* 26 (2012), 193–216.

47. Private, non-profit universities receive indirect state subsidies in the form of tax deductions for contributions, tax-free endowment income, lower property taxes, and the like.

48. Baum and Ma, *Trends in College Pricing 2014*, figure 19B (inflated to 2014 dollars).

CHAPTER 4: IS A CRISIS ON THE HORIZON?

1. "Troubling Student Loans," *New York Times*, April 28, 2014, accessed June 30, 2015, http://www.nytimes.com/2014/04/29/opinion/troubling-student-loans.html.

2. Bob Hildreth, "Will Student Loans Be the Next Mortgage Crisis?" *Boston Globe*, July 11, 2012, accessed June 30, 2015, https://www.boston globe.com/opinion/2012/07/11/will-student-loans-next-mortgage-crisis /kX55lAYy6ynllcahK0tRMN/story.html; Lizzie O'Leary, "Is Student Loan Debt the Next Housing Crisis?" *Marketplace*, August 30, 2013, accessed June 30, 2015, http://www.marketplace.org/topics/your-money/education /student-loan-debt-next-housing-crisis; Anthony Figliola, "Student Loans: America's Next Financial Crisis," *Huffington Post*, October 17, 2014, accessed June 30, 2015, http://www.huffingtonpost.com/anthony-figliola/student -loans-americas-next-financial-crisis_b_5999948.html.

3. The S&P/Case-Shiller housing price index peaked in 2006 but did not begin its precipitous decline until 2007 ("S&P/Case-Shiller 20-City Composite Home Price Index," Federal Reserve Bank of St. Louis, accessed June 30, 2015, https://research.stlouisfed.org/fred2/series/SPCS20RSA).

4. Martin Neil Baily, Robert E. Litan, and Matthew S. Johnson, "The Origins of the Financial Crisis," Brookings Institution, November 2008, accessed June 30, 2015, http://www.brookings.edu/~/media/research/files /papers/2008/11/origin-crisis-baily-litan/11_origins_crisis_baily_litan.pdf.

5. Baily, Litan, and Johnson, "The Origins of the Financial Crisis."

6. Anthony P. Carnevale, Stephen J. Rose, and Ban Cheah, "The College Payoff: Education, Occupations, Lifetime Earnings," Georgetown University Center on Education and the Workforce, August 5, 2011, accessed

July 1, 2015, https://cew.georgetown.edu/wp-content/uploads/2014/11/col legepayoff-complete.pdf.

7. Jason R. Abel and Richard Deitz, "Do the Benefits of College Still Outweigh the Costs?" *Current Issues in Economics and Finance* 20 (2014), accessed July 1, 2015, http://www.newyorkfed.org/research/current_issues /ci20-3.html.

8. Michael Greenstone and Adam Looney, "Regardless of the Cost, College Still Matters," Brookings Institution, October 2012, accessed January 5, 2016, http://www.brookings.edu/blogs/jobs/posts/2012/10/05-jobs -greenstone-looney.

9. For a review of the quasi-experimental evidence on the returns to education, see Seth Zimmerman, "The Returns to College Admission for Academically Marginal Students," *Journal of Labor Economics* 32 (2014): 711–754.

10. Brad Hershbein and Melissa S. Kearney, "Major Decisions: What Graduates Earn Over Their Lifetimes," Brookings Institution, September 2014, accessed July 2, 2015, http://www.hamiltonproject.org/papers/major _decisions_what_graduates_earn_over_their_lifetimes/.

11. Thomas Hungerford and Gary Solon, "Sheepskin Effects in the Returns to Education," *Review of Economics and Statistics* 69 (1987): 175–177.

12. Adam Looney and Constantine Yannelis, "A Crisis in Student Loans? How Changes in the Characteristics of Borrowers and the Institutions they Attended Contributed to Loan Defaults," *Brookings Papers on Economic Activity*, Conference Draft, September 2015, accessed January 6, 2016, http://www.brookings.edu/about/projects/bpea/papers/2015/looney -yannelis-student-loan-defaults, 5.

13. The data indicate that the increase in total debt is 3.2 times the increase in annual income, so the average household should be able to pay off the additional debt in 3.2 years, although in reality accounting for income taxes would modestly increase that estimate, by an amount that depends on the household's marginal tax rate.

14. In addition to wages, salaries, business income, and investment income, total income also includes unemployment, worker's compensation, child support, alimony, government benefits, disability benefits, and retirement programs.

15. For ease of exposition, this example makes a number of simplifying assumptions, including ignoring the time value of money (i.e., not discounting future payments) and not considering alternative investments. None of these simplifications alter our main conclusion.

16. Using lifetime income in the ratio instead of annual income produces a similar conclusion. In other words, the correct approach is not just to compare the stock of debt to the stock of earnings, although that is certainly

important, but also to compute the difference between these numbers rather than their ratio. The net profit on an investment (benefits minus costs) is much more informative than the rate of return on the investment (roughly speaking, the ratio of benefits to costs). This is similar to the problem of applying rates of return to different sized investments that we discussed above.

17. We exclude as likely data errors payment-to-income ratios greater than one. If we include these observations, as we have in previous work, we find that the mean ratio declined from 1992 to 2013 (Beth Akers and Matthew M. Chingos, "Is a Student Loan Crisis on the Horizon?" Brookings Institution, June 2014, accessed June 26, 2015, http://www.brookings.edu /research/reports/2014/06/24-student-loan-crisis-akers-chingos). The excluded observations are concentrated in the earlier survey years, which we interpret as implying that they are largely data errors and not instances of borrowers making student loan payments greater than income by drawing on savings.

18. Using total income, median payment-to-income ratios are mostly the same, whereas mean ratios are generally one percentage point lower than when we use wage income.

19. Authors' calculations from the Survey of Consumer Finances.

20. Authors' calculations from the Survey of Consumer Finances, based on the terms of the largest education loan held by each household.

21. U.S. Department of Education, "Cohort Default Rate Continues to Drop Across All Higher Ed Sectors," September 30, 2015, accessed January 6, 2016, http://www.ed.gov/news/press-releases/cohort-default-rate -continues-drop-across-all-higher-ed-sectors.

22. Looney and Yannelis, "A Crisis in Student Loans?" Figure 1 of their paper shows that their replicated two-year cohort default rates are somewhat higher than but generally track the official figures.

CHAPTER 5: HOW ARE STUDENT LOANS IMPACTING BORROWERS AND THE ECONOMY?

1. Annie Lowrey, "Student Debt Slows Growth as Young Spend Less," *New York Times*, May 10, 2013, accessed July 6, 2015, http://www.nytimes .com/2013/05/11/business/economy/student-loan-debt-weighing-down -younger-us-workers.html.

2. Dina ElBoghdady, "Student Debt May Hurt Housing Recovery by Hampering First-Time Buyers," *Washington Post*, February 17, 2014, accessed July 14, 2015, http://www.washingtonpost.com/business/economy /student-debt-may-hurt-housing-recovery-by-hampering-first-time-buyers

/2014/02/17/d90c7c1e-94bf-11e3-83b9-1f024193bb84_story.html; Meera Louis, "Student Debt Puts Young Entrepreneurs on Hold," *Bloomberg Business*, June 20, 2013, accessed July 6, 2015, http://www.bloomberg.com/bw/articles/2013-06-20/student-debt-puts-young-entrepreneurs-on-hold; Lowrey, "Student Debt Slows Growth."

3. In 1959, the top federal education official was unsure of how many women would take out newly available federal student loans because "No one knows how many girls would decide that a debt of $3,000 or $4,000 [$24,400 to $32,500 in 2014 dollars] might discourage a boy from marrying them" ("U.S. Fears Student Loan May Cost Girls Interest," *New York Times*, April 10, 1959, accessed July 14, 2015, http://query.nytimes.com/gst/abstract.html?res=9404E4DF1E3FE53BBC4852DFB2668382649EDE).

4. Andrew Dugan and Stephanie Kafka, "Student Debt Linked to Worse Health and Less Wealth," Gallup, August 7, 2014, accessed July 14, 2015, http://www.gallup.com/poll/174317/student-debt-linked-worse-health-less-wealth.aspx.

5. Meta Brown and Sydnee Caldwell, "Young Student Loan Borrowers Retreat from Housing and Auto Markets," Liberty Street Economics, Federal Reserve Bank of New York, April 17, 2013, accessed July 14, 2015, http://libertystreeteconomics.newyorkfed.org/2013/04/young-student-loan-borrowers-retreat-from-housing-and-auto-markets.html.

6. Lowrey, "Student Debt Slows Growth."

7. Researchers at both the Federal Reserve Board and the FRBNY are currently exploring this issue and have indicated that publications on this question are forthcoming.

8. Jason N. Houle and Lawrence M. Berger, "The End of the American Dream? Student Loan Debt and Homeownership Among Young Adults," *Third Way*, June 2, 2015, accessed October 1, 2015, http://thirdway.org/report/the-end-of-the-american-dream-student-loan-debt-and-home ownership-among-young-adults.

9. The latter explanation has also been considered by researchers at the Federal Reserve Bank of New York (Zachary Bleemer, Meta Brown, Donghoon Lee, and Wilbert van der Klaauw, "Debt, Jobs, or Housing: What's Keeping Millennials at Home?" *FRBNY Staff Reports*, September 2015, accessed October 1, 2015, http://newyorkfed.org/research/staff_reports/sr700.pdf).

10. Jesse Rothstein and Cecilia Elena Rouse, "Constrained after College: Student Loans and Early-Career Occupational Choices," *Journal of Public Economics* 95 (2011): 149–163.

11. Elizabeth Dwoskin, "Will You Marry Me (After I Pay Off My Student Loans)?" *Bloomberg Business*, March 28, 2012, accessed July 6, 2015,

http://www.bloomberg.com/bw/articles/2012–03–28/will-you-marry-me
-after-i-pay-off-my-student-loans.

12. Katrina M. Walsemann, Gilbert C. Gee, and Danielle Gentile, "Sick
of Our Loans: Student Borrowing and the Mental Health of Young Adults
in the United States," *Social Science and Medicine* 124 (2015): 85–93.

13. Rothstein and Rouse, "Constrained after College."

14. Susan Dynarski, "An Economist's Perspective on Student Loans in
the United States," Brookings Institution, September 2014, accessed July 15,
2015, http://www.brookings.edu/~/media/research/files/papers/2014/09
/economist_perspective_student_loans_dynarski/economist_perspective
_student_loans_dynarski.pdf.

15. Philip Oreopoulos and Uros Petronijevic, "Making College Worth
It: A Review of the Returns to Higher Education," *Future of Children* 23
(2013): 41–65.

16. Sandy Baum, Jennifer Ma, and Kathleen Payea, "Education Pay
2013: The Benefits of Higher Education for Individuals and Society," College Board, 2013, accessed July 15, 2015, http://trends.collegeboard.org
/sites/default/files/education-pays-2013-full-report-022714.pdf.

17. Walsemann et al., "Sick of Our Loans."

18. This concern also applies to education, which is potentially increased by taking on debt and was included as a control in the study.

19. For simplicity, we assume that the loan payment is made in
perpetuity.

20. "New York City Teacher Salary," NYC Department of Education,
accessed July 15, 2015, http://schools.nyc.gov/nr/rdonlyres/eddb658c-be7f
-4314–85c0–03f5a00b8a0b/0/salary.pdf.

CHAPTER 6: THE REAL PROBLEMS IN STUDENT LENDING

1. "National Student Loan Two-year Default Rates," U.S. Department
of Education, accessed July 6, 2015, https://www2.ed.gov/offices/OSFAP
/defaultmanagement/defaultrates.html.

2. Undergraduate students who are financially independent of their
parents, or whose parents were denied PLUS loans, are eligible to borrow a
lifetime maximum of $57,500 (see chapter 2).

3. Marian Wang, Beckie Supiano, and Andrea Fuller, "The Parent Loan
Trap," *Chronicle of Higher Education,* October 4, 2012, accessed July 6, 2015,
http://chronicle.com/article/The-Parent-Plus-Trap/134844.

4. Adam Looney and Constantine Yannelis, "A Crisis in Student Loans?
How Changes in the Characteristics of Borrowers and the Institutions they
Attended Contributed to Loan Defaults," *Brookings Papers on Economic Ac-*

tivity, Conference Draft, September 2015, accessed December 14, 2015, http://www.brookings.edu/~/media/projects/bpea/fall-2015_embargoed /conferencedraft_looneyyannelis_studentloandefaults.pdf, table 5.

5. Philip B. Levine, "Transparency in College Costs," Brookings Institution, November 2014, accessed July 6, 2015, http://www.brookings.edu /~/media/research/files/papers/2014/11/12-transparency-in-college-costs -levine/12_transparency_in_college_costs_levine.pdf.

6. The federal government also has data on the college attendance of non-borrowers through the 1098-T forms submitted by colleges to the IRS.

7. Clare McCann and Amy Laitinen, "College Blackout: How the Higher Education Lobby Fought to Keep Students in the Dark," New America, March 2014, accessed July 6, 2015, https://www.newamerica.org/down loads/CollegeBlackoutFINAL.pdf.

8. For a detailed discussion of the limitations of the new Scorecard data, see Grover J. Whitehurst and Matthew M. Chingos, "Deconstructing and Reconstructing the College Scorecard," Brookings Institution, October 2015, accessed December 15, 2015, http://www.brookings.edu/research /papers/2015/10/15-deconstructing-reconstructing-college-scorecard -whitehurst-chingos.

9. Calculations from "WG03: Institution and Program-specific Data," State Council of Higher Education for Virginia, accessed June 19, 2015, http://research.schev.edu/eom/opportunity03_report.asp.

10. Calculations from "WG03."

11. "Economic Success Metrics (ESM) Program," College Measures, accessed June 19, 2015, http://www.collegemeasures.org/esm/.

12. Healey Whitsett and Tom Allison, "College Information Design and Delivery—Insights from the Cognitive Information Processing Literature," Young Invincibles, May 2015, accessed December 15, 2015, http://young invincibles.org/wp-content/uploads/2015/06/college-information-design -5.28.2015-FINAL.pdf.

13. Elizabeth J. Akers and Matthew M. Chingos, "Are College Students Borrowing Blindly?" Brookings Institution, December 2014, accessed June 26, 2015, http://www.brookings.edu/~/media/research/files/reports/2014 /12/10-borrowing-blindly/are-college-students-borrowing-blindly_dec -2014.pdf.

14. Loans of program participants are forgiven after ten years for workers in the public and non-profit sectors.

15. Susan Dynarski and Daniel Kreisman, "Loans for Educational Opportunity: Making Borrowing Work for Today's Students," Hamilton Project, October 2013, accessed July 6, 2015, http://www.hamiltonproject.org /files/downloads_and_links/THP_DynarskiDiscPaper_Final.pdf.

16. Interest continues to accrue on all loans during forbearance ("Deferment and Forbearance," U.S. Department of Education, accessed July 6, 2015, https://studentaid.ed.gov/sa/repay-loans/deferment-forbearance).

17. "Income-Driven Plans," U.S. Department of Education, accessed December 15, 2015, https://studentaid.ed.gov/sa/repay-loans/understand/plans/income-driven.

18. Except for the ICR plan, where discretionary income is defined as income minus 100% of the federal poverty level.

19. Both of these calculations use the 2015 poverty guidelines for the 48 contiguous states and DC ("2015 Poverty Guidelines," U.S. Department of Health and Human Services, accessed June 19, 2015, http://www.aspe.hhs.gov/poverty/15poverty.cfm). Poverty levels are somewhat higher in Alaska and Hawaii, so borrowers in those states would face lower monthly payments under IDR.

20. The forgiven balance is treated as taxable income under current law, but we expect Congress to exclude loan forgiveness from taxable income before the first balances are forgiven, given that most individuals who qualify for forgiveness are unlikely to have the resources to pay this tax.

21. ICR caps payments at 20% of income and provides forgiveness after 25 years.

22. Shahien Nasiripour, "Education Department to Renew Sallie Mae Contract, Despite Allegations of Wrongdoing," *Huffington Post*, November 29, 2013, accessed July 6, 2015, http://www.huffingtonpost.com/2013/11/29/education-department-sallie-mae_n_4351509.html.

23. "The U.S. Department of Education's Administration of Student Loan Debt and Repayment: Final Audit Report," U.S. Department of Education Office of Inspector General, December 2014, accessed July 6, 2015, https://www2.ed.gov/about/offices/list/oig/auditreports/fy2015/a09n0011.pdf.

24. Eric M. Fink and Roland Zullo, "Federal Student Loan Servicing: Contract Problems and Public Solutions," Elon University and University of Michigan, June 2014, accessed July 6, 2015, https://www.elon.edu/docs/e-web/law/faculty/fink_zullo_federal_student_loan_servicing_report_06_25_2014.pdf.

25. Authors' analysis of 2014 Title IV Additional Servicing Contracts (2014) at "Loan Servicing Contracts," U.S. Department of Education, accessed June 19, 2015, https://studentaid.ed.gov/sa/about/data-center/business-info/contracts/loan-servicing.

26. Beth Akers, "How Much Is Too Much? Evidence on Financial Well-Being and Student Loan Debt," American Enterprise Institute, May 2014,

accessed July 6, 2015, https://www.aei.org/wp-content/uploads/2014/05
/-how-much-is-too-much_100837569045.pdf.

27. Meta Brown, Andrew Haughwout, Donghoon Lee, Joelle Scally,
and Wilbert van der Klaauw, "Looking at Student Loan Defaults through
a Larger Window," Liberty Street Economics blog, Federal Reserve Bank of
New York, February 19, 2015, accessed December 15, 2015, http://liberty
streeteconomics.newyorkfed.org/2015/02/looking_at_student_loan_de
faults_through_a_larger_window.html.

CHAPTER 7: SOLVING THE REAL PROBLEMS

1. Middle-income households had the highest debt levels—almost
$5,000 in 2014 dollars.

2. Including older households also captures those that took on education debt for their children. Among households age 20 and above, the top
fifth in terms of income held 39% of education debt in 1992.

3. Matt Phillips, "Why Elites Hate It When You Say Giant Student
Debts Aren't the Problem," *Quartz*, June 24, 2014, accessed July 7, 2015,
http://qz.com/225625/why-elites-hate-it-when-you-say-giant-student
-debts-arent-the-problem/.

4. Undergraduate borrowing also increased disproportionately among
students with higher-income parents between 1990 and 2012. See Matthew
M. Chingos, "Why Student Loan Rhetoric Doesn't Match the Facts," Brookings Institution, July 17, 2014, accessed July 7, 2015, http://www.brookings
.edu/research/papers/2014/07/17-student-loan-rhetoric-chingos.

5. Tamara Keith, "Fact Check: Is Refinancing Student Debt Really
Good Policy?" National Public Radio, December 17, 2015, accessed January 4, 2016, http://www.npr.org/sections/itsallpolitics/2015/08/21/433257
863/fact-check-is-refinancing-student-debt-really-good-policy.

6. Office of U.S. Senator Elizabeth Warren, "Floor Speech by Senator
Elizabeth Warren," February 12, 2014, accessed July 7, 2015, http://www
.warren.senate.gov/files/documents/2014-2-12%20Floor%20Speech%20
on%20Student%20Loans.pdf.

7. "Historical Interest Rates," FinAid, accessed July 7, 2015, http://
www.finaid.org/loans/historicalrates.phtml.

8. These calculations assume a ten-year repayment schedule. In reality, households in the SCF are at various stages of repayment (and have
various repayment terms), so this calculation is only illustrative.

9. All interest savings totals over the life of the loan are raw totals and
not discounted to the present.

10. For a discussion of how this might be accomplished, see Matthew M. Chingos, "End Government Profits on Student Loans: Shift Risk and Lower Interest Rates," Brookings Institution, April 30, 2015, accessed July 7, 2015, http://www.brookings.edu/researchpapers/2015/04/30-government-profit-loans-chingos.

11. Michael Grunwald, "The U.S. Government's Predatory-Lending Program," Politico, June 2015, accessed July 7, 2015, http://www.politico.com/agenda/story/2015/06/the-us-governments-predatory-lending-program-000094.

12. There is broad support among education policy analysts and advocacy groups for moving toward a single grant program and single loan program. See Libby A. Nelson, "Reimagining Financial Aid," Inside Higher Ed, March 14, 2013, accessed July 7, 2015, https://www.insidehighered.com/news/2013/03/14/look-all-15-reimagining-aid-design-and-delivery-reports-gates-foundation.

13. An alternative to automatic eligibility calculation based on income records is to use "prior-prior year" income data, which would enable students to apply for aid earlier than they can under the current system. For details, see National Association of Student Financial Aid Administrators, "Great Expectations: Implications of Implementing Prior-Prior Year Income Data for the FAFSA," May 2015, accessed July 7, 2015, http://www.nasfaa.org/uploads/documents/ektron/0af69743–833e-4eb3-b80a-fc1577104dfe/5df180059b0f4c6da9fd903764d16f823.pdf. The Department of Education began implementing this change in 2015. We believe that this is a step in the right direction, but that it doesn't go far enough.

14. For a detailed discussion of issues surrounding the calculation of living costs, see Robert Kelchen, Sara Goldrick-Rab, and Braden Hosch, "The Costs of College Attendance: Trends, Variation, and Accuracy in Institutional Living Cost Allowances" (paper presented at the annual meeting of the Association of Public Policy and Management, Albuquerque, New Mexico, November 6–8, 2014, http://wihopelab.com/publications/Kelchen%20Hosch%20Goldrick-Rab%202014.pdf).

15. Adam Looney and Constantine Yannelis, "A Crisis in Student Loans? How Changes in the Characteristics of Borrowers and the Institutions They Attended Contributed to Loan Defaults," Brookings Papers on Economic Activity, Conference Draft, September 2015, accessed December 14, 2015, http://www.brookings.edu/~/media/projects/bpea/fall-2015_embargoed/conferencedraft_looneyyannelis_studentloandefaults.pdf.

16. An important distinction between our proposal and the current income-driven repayment plans is that an automatic system would be based

on current income, not past income. For additional discussion of this issue, see Susan Dynarski, "The Trouble with Student Loans? Low Earnings, Not High Debt," Brookings Institution, January 2016, accessed January 16, 2016, http://www.brookings.edu/research/papers/2016/01/07-student-loans-low-earnings-dynarski.

17. For a detailed plan along these lines, see Susan Dynarski and Daniel Kreisman, "Loans for Educational Opportunity: Making Borrowing Work for Today's Students," Hamilton Project, October 2013, accessed July 6, 2015, http://www.hamiltonproject.org/files/downloads_and_links/THP_DynarskiDiscPaper_Final.pdf.

18. Danielle Douglas-Gabriel, "How the Attempt to Fix Student Loans Got Bogged Down by the Middlemen," Washington Post, August 23 2015, accessed January 6, 2016, https://www.washingtonpost.com/business/econ omy/how-the-education-department-turned-into-a-massive-bank/2015/08/23/7618f2fa-1442-11e5-9ddc-e3353542100c_story.html.

19. The Public Service Loan Forgiveness program, under which the remaining debts of participating borrowers working in the public and nonprofit sectors are forgiven after ten years, should be eliminated (for new borrowers, as we assume any changes would have to be). If policymakers wish to subsidize workers in certain sectors of the economy, they should do that directly (e.g., through tax credits) rather than through the student loan system.

20. Beth Akers and Matthew M. Chingos, "Student Loan Safety Nets: Estimating the Costs and Benefits of Income-Based Repayment," Brookings Institution, April 2014, accessed July 7, 2015, http://www.brookings.edu/research/papers/2014/04/14-income-based-repayment-akers-chingos.

21. Office of U.S. Senator Ron Wyden, "Wyden, Rubio, Warner Introduce "The Student Right to Know Before You Go Act," Office of U.S. Senator Ron Wyden, March 5, 2015, accessed July 7, 2015, http://www.wyden.senate.gov/news/press-releases/wyden-rubio-warner-introduce-the-student-right-to-know-before-you-go-act.

22. Office of U.S. Senator Marco Rubio, "Rubio, Warner Introduce Dynamic Student Loan Repayment Act," Office of U.S. Senator Marco Rubio, July 16, 2014, accessed July 7, 2015, http://www.rubio.senate.gov/public/index.cfm/press-releases?ID=21677deb-ff24-40a4-8033-b39d9a1ff26a.

23. "Financial Aid Simplification and Transparency (FAST) Act," accessed July 13, 2015, http://www.help.senate.gov/imo/media/doc/Final_draft_Onepager%20for%20fin%20aid%20bill%20with%20Bennet.pdf.

24. For an earlier free college proposal, see Sara Goldrick-Rab and Nancy Kendall, "Redefining College Affordability: Securing America's Future with

a Free Two Year College Option," Education Optimists, April 2014, accessed July 7, 2015, http://www.luminafoundation.org/files/publications/ideas _summit/Redefining_College_Affordability.pdf.

25. Michael Stratford, "Debt-Free Plans," *Inside Higher Ed*, June 19, 2015, accessed July 7, 2015, https://www.insidehighered.com/news/2015/06 /19/what-people-are-saying-about-debt-free.

26. At more selective public institutions, 44% of first-year students were from families in the top quarter of the income distribution, and 71% were from the top half. At less selective four-year public institutions, 31% were from the top quarter and 59% from the top half (William G. Bowen, Matthew M. Chingos, and Michael S. McPherson, *Crossing the Finish Line: Completing College at America's Public Universities* [Princeton: Princeton University Press, 2009], 141).

27. Henry J. Kaiser Family Foundation, "Current Status of State Medicaid Expansion Decisions," accessed January 17, 2016, http://kff.org/health -reform/slide/current-status-of-the-medicaid-expansion-decision/.

28. Sarah Cohodes and Joshua Goodman, "Merit Aid, College Quality and College Completion: Massachusetts' Adams Scholarship as an In-Kind Subsidy," *American Economic Journal: Applied Economics* 6 (2014): 251–285.

29. See Bowen et al., *Crossing the Finish Line*, 136–140, and evidence cited therein. For evidence that the negative effect of community college attendance varies across students, see Jennie E. Brand, Fabian T. Pfeffer, and Sara Goldrick-Rab, "The Community College Effect Revisited: The Importance of Attending to Heterogeneity and Complex Counterfactuals," California Center for Population Research, October 2014, accessed July 8, 2015, http://papers.ccpr.ucla.edu/papers/PWP-CCPR-2012-004/PWP-CCPR -2012-004.pdf.

30. "FACT SHEET—White House Unveils America's College Promise Proposal: Tuition-Free Community College for Responsible Students," White House Press Office, January 9, 2015, accessed July 7, 2015, https:// www.whitehouse.gov/the-press-office/2015/01/09/fact-sheet-white-house -unveils-america-s-college-promise-proposal-tuitio.

31. For a more detailed discussion of how to give colleges "skin in the game," see Andrew P. Kelly and Kevin James, "Untapped Potential: Making the Higher Education Market Work for Students and Taxpayers," American Enterprise Institute, October 2014, accessed July 7, 2015, https://www.aei .org/wp-content/uploads/2014/10/Untapped-Potential-corr.pdf.

32. For a lengthier discussion of ISAs, see Miguel Palacios, Tonio De-Sorrento, and Andrew P. Kelly, "Investing in Value, Sharing Risk: Financing Higher Education Through Income Share Agreements," American Enterprise Institute, February 2014, accessed July 8, 2015, https://www.aei.org

/wp-content/uploads/2014/02/-investing-in-value-sharing-in-risk-financing -higher-education-through-inome-share-agreements_083548906610.pdf.

33. Milton Friedman, "The Role of Government in Education (1955)," Friedman Foundation for Educational Choice, accessed July 6, 2015, http:// www.edchoice.org/The-Friedmans/The-Friedmans-on-School-Choice /The-Role-of-Government-in-Education-(1995).aspx.

34. Jason Delisle, "What Does Income-based Repayment for Student Loans Cost?" New America, May 21, 2015, accessed July 8, 2015, http:// www.edcentral.org/income-based-repayment-cost/.

References

Abel, Jason R., and Richard Deitz. "Do the Benefits of College Still Outweigh the Costs?" *Current Issues in Economics and Finance* 20 (2014). Accessed July 1, 2015. http://www.newyorkfed.org/research/current_issues/ci20-3.html.

Akers, Beth. "How Much Is Too Much? Evidence on Financial Well-Being and Student Loan Debt." American Enterprise Institute, May 2014. Accessed July 6, 2015. https://www.aei.org/wp-content/uploads/2014/05/-how-much-is-too-much_100837569045.pdf.

Akers, Beth, and Matthew M. Chingos. "Is a Student Loan Crisis on the Horizon?" Brookings Institution, June 2014. Accessed June 26, 2015. http://www.brookings.edu/research/reports/2014/06/24-student-loan-crisis-akers-chingos.

Akers, Beth, and Matthew M. Chingos. "Student Loan Safety Nets: Estimating the Costs and Benefits of Income-Based Repayment." Brookings Institution, April 2014. Accessed July 7, 2015. http://www.brookings.edu/research/papers/2014/04/14-income-based-repayment-akers-chingos.

Akers, Elizabeth J., and Matthew M. Chingos. "Are College Students Borrowing Blindly?" Brookings Institution, December 2014. Accessed June 26, 2015. http://www.brookings.edu/~/media/research/files/reports/2014/12/10-borrowing-blindly/are-college-students-borrowing-blindly_dec-2014.pdf.

Associated Press. "63,000 Delinquent on Student Loans," April 10, 1982. Accessed July 6, 2015. http://www.nytimes.com/1982/04/10/us/63000-delinquent-on-student-loans.html.

Bailey, Martha J., and Susan M. Dynarski. "Gains and Gaps: Changing Inequality in U.S. College Entry and Completion." National Bureau of Economic Research Working Paper No. 17633, December 2011.

Baily, Martin Neil, Robert E. Litan, and Matthew S. Johnson. "The Origins of the Financial Crisis." Brookings Institution, November 2008. Accessed

June 30, 2015. http://www.brookings.edu/~/media/research/files/papers/2008/11/origin-crisis-baily-litan/11_origins_crisis_baily_litan.pdf.

Baum, Sandy, David W. Breneman, Matthew M. Chingos, Ronald G. Ehrenberg, Pamela Fowler, John Hayek, Donald E. Heller, Allison G. Jones, David A. Longanecker, Tim Nesbitt, Judith Scott-Clayton, Sarah E. Turner, Jane V. Wellman, and Grover "Russ" Whitehurst. "Beyond Need and Merit: Strengthening State Grant Programs." Brown Center on Education Policy, Brookings Institution, May 2012. Accessed October 6, 2015. http://www.brookings.edu/~/media/research/files/reports/2012/5/08%20grants%20chingos%20whitehurst/0508_state_grant_chingos_whitehurst.pdf.

Baum, Sandy, Diane Cardenas Elliott, and Jennifer Ma. *Trends in Student Aid 2014.* New York: College Board, 2014. Accessed June 26, 2015. https://secure-media.collegeboard.org/digitalServices/misc/trends/2014-trends-student-aid-report-final.pdf

Baum, Sandy, and Jennifer Ma, *Trends in College Pricing 2014.* New York: College Board, 2014. Accessed June 26, 2015. https://secure-media.collegeboard.org/digitalServices/misc/trends/2014-trends-college-pricing-report-final.pdf.

Baum, Sandy, Jennifer Ma, and Kathleen Payea. "Education Pay 2013: The Benefits of Higher Education for Individuals and Society." College Board, 2013. Accessed July 15, 2015. http://trends.collegeboard.org/sites/default/files/education-pays-2013-full-report-022714.pdf.

Baumol, William, and William Bowen. *Performing Arts, The Economic Dilemma: A Study of Problems Common to Theater, Opera, Music, and Dance.* New York: Twentieth Century Fund, 1966.

Bleemer, Zachary, Meta Brown, Donghoon Lee, and Wilbert van der Klaauw. "Debt, Jobs, or Housing: What's Keeping Millennials at Home?" *FRBNY Staff Reports,* September 2015. Accessed October 1, 2015. http://newyorkfed.org/research/staff_reports/sr700.pdf.

Bowen, William G., Matthew M. Chingos, and Michael S. McPherson. *Crossing the Finish Line: Completing College at America's Public Universities.* Princeton: Princeton University Press, 2009.

Brand, Jennie E., Fabian T. Pfeffer, and Sara Goldrick-Rab. "The Community College Effect Revisited: The Importance of Attending to Heterogeneity and Complex Counterfactuals." California Center for Population Research, October 2014. Accessed July 8, 2015. http://papers.ccpr.ucla.edu/papers/PWP-CCPR-2012-004/PWP-CCPR-2012-004.pdf.

Brown, Meta, and Sydnee Caldwell. "Young Student Loan Borrowers Retreat from Housing and Auto Markets." Liberty Street Economics, Federal Reserve Bank of New York, April 17, 2013. Accessed July 14, 2015.

http://libertystreeteconomics.newyorkfed.org/2013/04/young-student
-loan-borrowers-retreat-from-housing-and-auto-markets.html.

Brown, Meta, Andrew Haughwout, Donghoon Lee, Joelle Scally, and Wilbert van der Klaauw. "Looking at Student Loan Defaults through a Larger Window." Liberty Street Economics blog, Federal Reserve Bank of New York, February 19, 2015. Accessed December 15, 2015. http://libertystreeteconomics.newyorkfed.org/2015/02/looking_at_student_loan_defaults_through_a_larger_window.html.

Bulman, George B., and Caroline M. Hoxby. "The Returns to the Federal Tax Credits for Higher Education." National Bureau of Economic Research Working Paper No. 20833, January 2015.

Carnevale, Anthony P., Stephen J. Rose, and Ban Cheah. "The College Payoff: Education, Occupations, Lifetime Earnings." Georgetown University Center on Education and the Workforce, August 5, 2011. Accessed July 1, 2015. https://cew.georgetown.edu/wp-content/uploads/2014/11/college payoff-complete.pdf.

Caro, Robert A. The Years of Lyndon Johnson: The Path to Power. New York: Knopf, 1982.

Cellini, Stephanie Riegg, and Claudia Goldin. "Does Federal Student Aid Raise Tuition? New Evidence on For-Profit Colleges." American Economic Journal: Economic Policy 6 (2014): 174–206.

Chingos, Matthew M. "Why Student Loan Rhetoric Doesn't Match the Facts." Brookings Institution, July 17, 2014. Accessed July 7, 2015. http://www.brookings.edu/research/papers/2014/07/17-student-loan-rhetoric-chingos.

Chingos, Matthew M. "End Government Profits on Student Loans: Shift Risk and Lower Interest Rates." Brookings Institution, April 30, 2015. Accessed July 7, 2015. http://www.brookings.edu/research/papers/2015/04/30-government-profit-loans-chingos.

Chopra, Rohit. "Too Big to Fail: Student Debt Hit a Trillion." Consumer Financial Protection Bureau, March 21, 2012. Accessed July 6, 2015. http://www.consumerfinance.gov/blog/too-big-to-fail-student-debt-hits-a-trillion/.

Chopra, Rohit. "Annual Report of the CFPB Student Loan Ombudsman." Consumer Financial Protection Bureau, October 16, 2014. Accessed June 26, 2015. http://files.consumerfinance.gov/f/201410_cfpb_report_annual-report-of-the-student-loan-ombudsman.pdf.

Cohodes, Sarah, and Joshua Goodman. "Merit Aid, College Quality and College Completion: Massachusetts' Adams Scholarship as an In-Kind Subsidy." American Economic Journal: Applied Economics 6 (2014): 251–285.

College Board. "Percentage of Undergraduate and Graduate Students Borrowing Private Loans over Time." Accessed June 26, 2015. http://trends.collegeboard.org/student-aid/figures-tables/percentage-undergraduate-and-graduate-students-borrowing-private-loans-over-time.

College Board. "Total Federal and Nonfederal Loans over Time." Accessed June 26, 2015. http://trends.collegeboard.org/student-aid/figures-tables/total-federa-nonfederal-loans-time.

College Measures. "Economic Success Metrics (ESM) Program." Accessed June 19, 2015. http://www.collegemeasures.org/esm/.

Consumer Financial Protection Bureau. "Private Student Loans." August 29, 2012. Accessed June 26, 2015. http://files.consumerfinance.gov/f/201207_cfpb_Reports_Private-Student-Loans.pdf.

Davidson, Adam. "It's Official: The Boomerang Kids Won't Leave." New York Times, June 20, 2014. Accessed June 26, 2015. http://www.nytimes.com/slideshow/2014/06/22/magazine/22boomerang_ss-nytnowcopy.html.

Delisle, Jason. "What Does Income-based Repayment for Student Loans Cost?" New America, May 21, 2015. Accessed July 8, 2015. http://www.edcentral.org/income-based-repayment-cost/.

Douglas-Gabriel, Danielle. "How the Attempt to Fix Student Loans Got Bogged Down by the Middlemen." Washington Post, August 23 2015. Accessed January 6, 2016. https://www.washingtonpost.com/business/economy/how-the-education-department-turned-into-a-massive-bank/2015/08/23/7618f2fa-1442-11e5-9ddc-e3353542100c_story.html.

Dugan, Andrew, and Stephanie Kafka. "Student Debt Linked to Worse Health and Less Wealth." Gallup, August 7, 2014. Accessed July 14, 2015. http://www.gallup.com/poll/174317/student-debt-linked-worse-health-less-wealth.aspx.

Dwoskin, Elizabeth. "Will You Marry Me (After I Pay Off My Student Loans)?" Bloomberg Business, March 28, 2012. Accessed July 6, 2015. http://www.bloomberg.com/bw/articles/2012-03-28/will-you-marry-me-after-i-pay-off-my-student-loans.

Dynarski, Susan. "An Economist's Perspective on Student Loans in the United States." Brookings Institution, September 2014. Accessed July 15, 2015. http://www.brookings.edu/~/media/research/files/papers/2014/09/economist_perspective_student_loans_dynarski/economist_perspective_student_loans_dynarski.pdf.

Dynarski, Susan. "We're Frighteningly in the Dark About Student Debt," New York Times, March 20, 2015. Accessed June 26, 2015. http://www.nytimes.com/2015/03/22/upshot/were-frighteningly-in-the-dark-about-student-debt.html.

Dynarski, Susan. "The Trouble with Student Loans? Low Earnings, Not High Debt." Brookings Institution, January 2016. Accessed January 16, 2016. http://www.brookings.edu/research/papers/2016/01/07-student-loans -low-earnings-dynarski.

Dynarski, Susan, and Daniel Kreisman. "Loans for Educational Opportunity: Making Borrowing Work for Today's Students." Hamilton Project, October 2013. Accessed July 6, 2015. http://www.hamiltonproject.org /files/downloads_and_links/THP_DynarskiDiscPaper_Final.pdf.

Ehrenberg, Ronald G. "American Higher Education in Transition." *Journal of Economic Perspectives* 26 (2012): 193–216.

ElBoghdady, Dina. "Student Debt May Hurt Housing Recovery by Hampering First-Time Buyers." *Washington Post*, February 17, 2014. Accessed July 14, 2015. http://www.washingtonpost.com/business/economy/stu dent-debt-may-hurt-housing-recovery-by-hampering-first-time-buyers /2014/02/17/d90c7c1e-94bf-11e3-83b9-1f024193bb84_story.html.

Federal Reserve Bank of New York. "2015 Q1 Report." Accessed July 9, 2015. http://www.newyorkfed.org/microeconomics/data.html.

Federal Reserve Bank of St. Louis. "S&P/Case-Shiller 20-City Composite Home Price Index," Accessed June 30, 2015. https://research.stlouisfed .org/fred2/series/SPCS20RSA.

Figliola, Anthony. "Student Loans: America's Next Financial Crisis." *Huffington Post*, October 17, 2014. Accessed June 30, 2015. http://www.huff ingtonpost.com/anthony-figliola/student-loans-americas-next-financial -crisis_b_5999948.html.

FinAid. "History of Student Financial Aid." Accessed June 26, 2015. http:// www.finaid.org/educators/history.phtml.

FinAid. "Historical Interest Rates." Accessed July 7, 2015. http://www.finaid .org/loans/historicalrates.phtml.

FinAid. "Student Loan Debt Clock." Accessed December 14, 2015. http:// www.finaid.org/loans/studentloandebtclock.phtml.

Fink, Eric M., and Roland Zullo. "Federal Student Loan Servicing: Contract Problems and Public Solutions." Elon University and University of Michigan, June 2014. Accessed July 6, 2015. https://www.elon.edu/docs/e -web/law/faculty/fink_zullo_federal_student_loan_servicing_report _06_25_2014.pdf.

Fishman, Rachel. "The Parent Trap: Parent PLUS Loans and Intergenerational Borrowing." *New America*, January 2014. Accessed June 26, 2015. https://static.newamerica.org/attachments/748-the-parent-trap/Cor rected-20140110-ParentTrap.pdf.

Friedman, Milton. "The Role of Government in Education (1955)." Friedman Foundation for Educational Choice. Accessed July 6, 2015. http://

www.edchoice.org/The-Friedmans/The-Friedmans-on-School-Choice
/The-Role-of-Government-in-Education-(1995).aspx.

Ginsburg, Benjamin. *The Fall of the Faculty: The Rise of the All-Administrative University and Why It Matters.* Oxford: Oxford University Press, 2011.

Gladieux, Lawrence E. "Federal Student Aid Policy: A History and an Assessment." *Financing Postsecondary Education: The Federal Role— October 1995.* U.S. Department of Education. Accessed December 14, 2015. https://www2.ed.gov/offices/OPE/PPI/FinPostSecEd/gladieux.html.

Goldrick-Rab, Sara, and Nancy Kendall. "Redefining College Affordability: Securing America's Future with a Free Two Year College Option." Education Optimists, April 2014. Accessed July 7, 2015. http://www.lumina foundation.org/files/publications/ideas_summit/Redefining_College _Affordability.pdf.

Greenstone, Michael, and Adam Looney. "Regardless of the Cost, College Still Matters." Brookings Institution, October 2012. Accessed January 5, 2016. http://www.brookings.edu/blogs/jobs/posts/2012/10/05-jobs-green stone-looney.

Grunwald, Michael. "The U.S. Government's Predatory-Lending Program." *Politico*, June 2015. Accessed July 7, 2015. http://www.politico .com/agenda/story/2015/06/the-us-governments-predatory-lending -program-000094.

Hansen, Janet S. "The Politics of Federal Scholarships: A Case Study of the Development of General Grant Assistance for Undergraduates." PhD diss., Princeton University, 1977.

Hansen, Janet S. *Student Loans: Are They Overburdening a Generation?* New York: College Board, 1987.

Harmon Foundation. "Seven Years' Experience with Student Loans." New York: Harmon Foundation, 1929.

Henry J. Kaiser Family Foundation. "Current Status of State Medicaid Expansion Decisions." Accessed January 17, 2016. http://kff.org/health -reform/slide/current-status-of-the-medicaid-expansion-decision/.

Hershbein, Brad, and Kevin M. Hollenbeck. "The Distribution of College Graduate Debt, 1990–2008: A Decomposition Approach." In *Student Loans and the Dynamics of Debt*, edited by Brad Hershbein and Kevin M. Hollenbeck, 53–116. Kalamazoo, MI: W. E. Upjohn Institute for Employment Research, 2015.

Hershbein, Brad, and Melissa S. Kearney. "Major Decisions: What Graduates Earn Over Their Lifetimes." Brookings Institution, September 2014. Accessed July 2, 2015. http://www.hamiltonproject.org/papers/major _decisions_what_graduates_earn_over_their_lifetimes/.

Hildreth, Bob. "Will Student Loans Be the Next Mortgage Crisis?" *Boston Globe*, July 11, 2012. Accessed June 30, 2015. https://www.bostonglobe.com/opinion/2012/07/11/will-student-loans-next-mortgage-crisis/kX55lAYy6ynllcahK0tRMN/story.html.

Horn, Laura, and Jonathan Paslov. "Trends in Student Financing of Undergraduate Education: Selected Years, 1995–96 to 2011–12." U.S. Department of Education, September 2014. Accessed June 26, 2015. http://nces.ed.gov/pubs2014/2014013rev.pdf.

Houle, Jason N., and Lawrence M. Berger. "The End of the American Dream? Student Loan Debt and Homeownership among Young Adults." *Third Way*, June 2, 2015. Accessed October 1, 2015. http://thirdway.org/report/the-end-of-the-american-dream-student-loan-debt-and-home ownership-among-young-adults.

Hungerford, Thomas, and Gary Solon. "Sheepskin Effects in the Returns to Education." *Review of Economics and Statistics* 69 (1987): 175–177.

Jacob, Brian, Brian McCall, and Kevin M. Stange. "College as Country Club: Do Colleges Cater to Students' Preferences for Consumption?" National Bureau of Economic Research Working Paper No. 18745, 2013.

Kane Thomas J., Peter R. Orszag, and David L. Gunter, "State Fiscal Constraints and Higher Education Spending: The Role of Medicaid and the Business Cycle," Urban-Brookings Tax Policy Center Discussion Paper No. 11, May 2003.

Keith, Tamara. "Fact Check: Is Refinancing Student Debt Really Good Policy?" *NPR*, December 17, 2015. Accessed January 4, 2016. http://www.npr.org/sections/itsallpolitics/2015/08/21/433257863/fact-check-is-refinancing-student-debt-really-good-policy.

Kelchen, Robert, Sara Goldrick-Rab, and Braden Hosch. "The Costs of College Attendance: Trends, Variation, and Accuracy in Institutional Living Cost Allowances." Paper presented at the annual meeting of the Association of Public Policy and Management, Albuquerque, New Mexico, November 6–8, 2014.

Kelly, Andrew P., and Kevin James. "Untapped Potential: Making the Higher Education Market Work for Students and Taxpayers." American Enterprise Institute, October 2014. Accessed July 7, 2015. https://www.aei.org/wp-content/uploads/2014/10/Untapped-Potential-corr.pdf.

Lederman, Doug. "How Americans Pay for College." *Inside Higher Ed*, August 20, 2008. Accessed December 7, 2015. https://www.insidehighered.com/news/2008/08/20/pay.

Levine, Philip B. "Transparency in College Costs." Brookings Institution, November 2014. Accessed July 6, 2015. http://www.brookings.edu/~

/media/research/files/papers/2014/11/12-transparency-in-college-costs
-levine/12_transparency_in_college_costs_levine.pdf.

Long, Bridget Terry. "How Do Financial Aid Policies Affect Colleges? The Institutional Impact of the Georgia HOPE Scholarship." *Journal of Human Resources* 39 (2004): 1045–1066.

Looney, Adam, and Constantine Yannelis. "A Crisis in Student Loans? How Changes in the Characteristics of Borrowers and the Institutions they Attended Contributed to Loan Defaults." *Brookings Papers on Economic Activity*, Conference Draft, September 2015. Accessed December 14, 2015. http://www.brookings.edu/~/media/projects/bpea/fall-2015_embar goed/conferencedraft_looneyyannelis_studentloandefaults.pdf.

Louis, Meera. "Student Debt Puts Young Entrepreneurs on Hold." *Bloomberg Business*, June 20, 2013. Accessed July 6, 2015, http://www.bloomberg .com/bw/articles/2013-06-20/student-debt-puts-young-entrepreneurs -on-hold.

Lowrey, Annie. "Student Debt Slows Growth as Young Spend Less." *New York Times*, May 10, 2013. Accessed July 6, 2015. http://www.nytimes .com/2013/05/11/business/economy/student-loan-debt-weighing -down-younger-us-workers.html.

Lucca, David O., Taylor Nadauld, and Karen Shen. "Credit Supply and the Rise in College Tuition: Evidence from the Expansion in Federal Student Aid Programs." Federal Reserve Bank of New York Staff Report No. 733, July 2015. Accessed July 9, 2015. http://www.newyorkfed.org/research /staff_reports/sr733.pdf.

Lumina Foundation. "How Did We Get Here: Growth of Federal Student Loans (Part 1)." YouTube. Accessed June 26, 2015. https://www.youtube .com/watch?v=6Cha6bWhuD0.

Lyndon Baines Johnson Presidential Library. "Education Timeline for 1963–1968." Accessed June 26, 2015. http://www.lbjlib.utexas.edu/johnson/lbj forkids/edu_timeline.shtm.

Martin, Andrew, and Andrew W. Lehren. "A Generation Hobbled by the Soaring Cost of College." *New York Times*, May 12, 2012. Accessed June 26, 2015. http://www.nytimes.com/2012/05/13/business/student-loans -weighing-down-a-generation-with-heavy-debt.html.

McCann, Clare, and Amy Laitinen. "College Blackout: How the Higher Education Lobby Fought to Keep Students in the Dark." *New America*, March 2014. Accessed July 6, 2015. https://www.newamerica.org/downloads /CollegeBlackoutFINAL.pdf.

McDonald, Matt, and Pat Brady. "The Plural of Anecdote Is Data (Except for Student Debt)." Hamilton Place Strategies. Accessed June 26, 2015.

http://hamiltonplacestrategies.com/sites/default/files/newsfiles/Media
%20coverage%20of%20student%20debt_1.pdf.

MeasureOne. "The MeasureOne Student Loan Performance Report Q3
2014." Accessed June 26, 2015. http://www.measureone.com/system/tdf
/reports/MeasureOne%20Private%20Student%20Loan%20Performance
%20Report%20Q3%202014%20121614%20FINAL.pdf?file=1.

Monro, John U. "Untapped Resource: Loans for Student Aid." *College Board
Review* Winter (1956): 14–18.

Nasiripour, Shahien. "Education Department to Renew Sallie Mae Contract, Despite Allegations of Wrongdoing." *Huffington Post*, November
29, 2013. Accessed July 6, 2015. http://www.huffingtonpost.com/2013
/11/29/education-department-sallie-mae_n_4351509.html.

National Association of Student Financial Aid Administrators. "Great Expectations: Implications of Implementing Prior-Prior Year Income Data
for the FAFSA." May 2015. Accessed July 7, 2015. http://www.nasfaa.org
/uploads/documents/ektron/0af69743-833e-4eb3-b80a-fc1577104dfe
/5df180059b0f4c6da9fd903764d16f823.pdf.

Nelson, Libby A. "Reimagining Financial Aid." *Inside Higher Ed*, March 14,
2013. Accessed July 7, 2015. https://www.insidehighered.com/news
/2013/03/14/look-all-15-reimagining-aid-design-and-delivery-reports
gates-foundation.

New York City Department of Education. "New York City Teacher Salary."
Accessed July 15, 2015. http://schools.nyc.gov/nr/rdonlyres/eddb658c
-be7f-4314-85c0-03f5a00b8a0b/0/salary.pdf.

Office of U.S. Senator Marco Rubio. "Rubio, Warner Introduce Dynamic
Student Loan Repayment Act." July 16, 2014. Accessed July 7, 2015.
http://www.rubio.senate.gov/public/index.cfm/press-releases?ID
=21677deb-ff24-40a4-8033-b39d9a1ff26a.

Office of U.S. Senator Elizabeth Warren. "Floor Speech by Senator Elizabeth Warren." February 12, 2014. Accessed July 7, 2015. http://www.war
ren.senate.gov/files/documents/2014-2-12%20Floor%20Speech%20
on%20Student%20Loans.pdf.

Office of U.S. Senator Ron Wyden. "Wyden, Rubio, Warner Introduce 'The
Student Right to Know Before You Go Act.'" March 5, 2015. Accessed
July 7, 2015. http://www.wyden.senate.gov/news/press-releases/wyden
-rubio-warner-introduce-the-student-right-to-know-before-you-go-act.

O'Leary, Lizzie. "Is Student Loan Debt the Next Housing Crisis?" *Marketplace*, August 30, 2013. Accessed June 30, 2015. http://www.marketplace
.org/topics/your-money/education/student-loan-debt-next-housing
-crisis.

Oreopoulos, Philip, and Uros Petronijevic. "Making College Worth It: A Review of the Returns to Higher Education." *Future of Children* 23 (2013): 41–65.

Palacios, Miguel, Tonio DeSorrento, and Andrew P. Kelly. "Investing in Value, Sharing Risk: Financing Higher Education Through Income Share Agreements." American Enterprise Institute, February 2014. Accessed July 8, 2015. https://www.aei.org/wp-content/uploads/2014/02/-invest ing-in-value-sharing-in-risk-financing-higher-education-through-in ome-share-agreements_083548906610.pdf.

Patton, Stacey. "A Graduate Student With $88,000 in Student Loans Speaks Out About College Debt." *Chronicle of Higher Education*, March 19, 2012. Accessed June 26, 2015. http://chronicle.com/article/A-Graduate -Student-With/131251/.

Phillips, Matt. "Why Elites Hate It When You Say Giant Student Debts Aren't the Problem." *Quartz*, June 24, 2014. Accessed July 7, 2015. http:// qz.com/225625/why-elites-hate-it-when-you-say-giant-student-debts -arent-the-problem/.

Radford, Alexandria Walton, Lutz Berkner, Sara C. Wheeless, and Bryan Shepherd. "Persistence and Attainment of 2003–04 Beginning Postsec- ondary Students: After 6 Years." National Center for Education Statistics, December 2010. Accessed January 9, 2016. http://nces.ed.gov/pubs2011 /2011151.pdf.

Rothstein, Jesse, and Cecilia Elena Rouse. "Constrained After College: Stu- dent Loans and Early-Career Occupational Choices." *Journal of Public Economics* 95 (2011): 149–163.

Spivak, Jonathan. "Higher Education Act of 1965, to Be Signed Today, Extends Federal Aid to New Areas." *Wall Street Journal*, November 8, 1965, 4.

State Council of Higher Education for Virginia. "WG03: Institution and Program-specific Data." Accessed June 19, 2015. http://research.schev .edu/eom/opportunity03_report.asp.

Stratford, Michael. "Debt-Free Plans." *Inside Higher Ed*, June 19, 2015. Ac- cessed July 7, 2015. https://www.insidehighered.com/news/2015/06/19 /what-people-are-saying-about-debt-free.

"Troubling Student Loans." Special to the *New York Times*, April 28, 2014. Accessed June 30, 2015. http://www.nytimes.com/2014/04/29/opinion /troubling-student-loans.html.

Turner, Lesley J. "The Road to Pell Is Paved with Good Intentions: The Eco- nomic Incidence of Federal Student Grant Aid." University of Maryland, August 14, 2014. Accessed January 9, 2016. http://econweb.umd.edu /~turner/Turner_FedAidIncidence.pdf.

Turner, Nicholas. "Who Benefits from Student Aid? The Economic Incidence of Tax-Based Federal Student Aid." *Economics of Education Review* 31 (2012): 463–481.

U.S. Bureau of Labor Statistics. "Earnings and Unemployment Rates by Educational Attainment." Accessed July 1, 2015. http://www.bls.gov/emp /ep_chart_001.htm.

U.S. Department of Education. "Cohort Default Rate Continues to Drop Across All Higher Ed Sectors." September 30, 2015. Accessed January 6, 2016. http://www.ed.gov/news/press-releases/cohort-default-rate-continues -drop-across-all-higher-ed-sectors.

U.S. Department of Education. "Deferment and Forbearance." Accessed June 26, 2015. https://studentaid.ed.gov/repay-loans/deferment-forbearance.

U.S. Department of Education. "Direct PLUS Loans and Adverse Credit." Accessed June 26, 2015. https://studentaid.ed.gov/sites/default/files/plus -adverse-credit.pdf.

U.S. Department of Education. "Federal Student Loan Portfolio." Accessed December 14, 2015. https://studentaid.ed.gov/about/data-center/student /portfolio.

U.S. Department of Education. "Income-Driven Plans." Accessed December 15, 2015. https://studentaid.ed.gov/sa/repay-loans/understand/plans /income-driven.

U.S. Department of Education. "Loan Servicing Contracts." Accessed June 19, 2015. https://studentaid.ed.gov/sa/about/data-center/business-info /contracts/loan-servicing.

U.S. Department of Education. "National Student Loan Two-year Default Rates." Accessed July 6, 2015. https://www2.ed.gov/offices/OSFAP/de faultmanagement/defaultrates.html.

U.S. Department of Education. "Repayment Plans." Accessed June 26, 2015. https://studentaid.ed.gov/repay-loans/understand/plans.

U.S. Department of Education. "Standard Plan." Accessed June 26, 2015. https://studentaid.ed.gov/repay-loans/understand/plans/standard.

U.S. Department of Education. "Who Gets Aid." Accessed June 26, 2015. https://studentaid.ed.gov/eligibility.

U.S. Department of Education Office of Inspector General. "The U.S. Department of Education's Administration of Student Loan Debt and Repayment: Final Audit Report." December 2014. Accessed July 6, 2015. https://www2.ed.gov/about/offices/list/oig/auditreports/fy2015/a09n 0011.pdf.

U.S. Department of Health and Human Services. "2015 Poverty Guidelines." Accessed June 19, 2015. http://www.aspe.hhs.gov/poverty/15pov erty.cfm.

"U.S. Fears Student Loan May Cost Girls Interest." Special to the *New York Times*, April 10, 1959. Accessed July 14, 2015. http://query.nytimes.com/gst/abstract.html?res=9404E4DF1E3FE53BBC4852DFB2668382649EDE.

U.S. Senate Committee on Health, Education, Labor, and Pensions. "Financial Aid Simplification and Transparency (FAST) Act." Accessed July 13, 2015. http://www.help.senate.gov/imo/media/doc/Final_draft_Onepager%20for%20fin%20aid%20bill%20with%20Bennet.pdf.

Walsemann, Katrina M., Gilbert C. Gee, and Danielle Gentile. "Sick of Our Loans: Student Borrowing and the Mental Health of Young Adults in the United States." *Social Science and Medicine* 124 (2015): 85–93.

Wang, Marian, Beckie Supiano, and Andrea Fuller. "The Parent Loan Trap." *Chronicle of Higher Education*, October 4, 2012. Accessed July 6, 2015. http://chronicle.com/article/The-Parent-Plus-Trap/134844.

Weisman, Steven R. "Reagan Attacks Critics Over Cut in Student Aid." *New York Times*, April 11, 1982. Accessed July 6, 2015. http://www.nytimes.com/1982/04/11/us/reagan-attacks-critics-over-cut-in-student-aid.html.

White House Press Office. "FACT SHEET—White House Unveils America's College Promise Proposal: Tuition-Free Community College for Responsible Students." January 9, 2015. Accessed July 7, 2015. https://www.whitehouse.gov/the-press-office/2015/01/09/fact-sheet-white-house-unveils-america-s-college-promise-proposal-tuitio.

Whitehurst, Grover J., and Matthew M. Chingos. "Deconstructing and Reconstructing the College Scorecard." Brookings Institution, October 2015. Accessed December 15, 2015. http://www.brookings.edu/research/papers/2015/10/15-deconstructing-reconstructing-college-scorecard-whitehurst-chingos.

Whitsett, Healey, and Tom Allison. "College Information Design and Delivery—Insights from the Cognitive Information Processing Literature." Young Invincibles, May 2015. Accessed December 15, 2015. http://younginvincibles.org/wp-content/uploads/2015/06/college-information-design-5.28.2015-FINAL.pdf.

Wilkinson, Rupert. *Aiding Students, Buying Students: Financial Aid in America*. Nashville, TN: Vanderbilt University Press, 2005.

Woo, Jennie H., and Stacy Shaw. "Trends in Graduate Student Financing: Selected Years, 1995–96 to 2011–12." U.S. Department of Education, January 2015. Accessed June 26, 2015. http://nces.ed.gov/pubs2015/2015026.pdf.

Zimmerman, Seth. "The Returns to College Admission for Academically Marginal Students." *Journal of Labor Economics* 32 (2014): 711–754.

Index

Note: Page numbers in *italics* indicate illustrations; those with a *t* indicate tables.